Pro
Côte

CW01667009

Claude Hervé-Bazin

JPMGUIDES

Contents

This Way Provence	**3**
Flashback	**6**
On the Scene	**13**
Avignon and region	**13**
Alpilles, Luberon and Haute-Provence	**25**
Camargue	**37**
Marseille and region	**45**
Côte d'Azur: Cassis to Hyères	**53**
Le Lavandou to l'Esterel	**59**
Cannes to Menton	**65**
Cultural Notes	**84**
Shopping	**86**
Dining Out	**87**
Sports	**90**
The Hard Facts	**92**
Index	104

Maps

Aix-en-Provence 96
Avignon 97, Marseille 98–99
Cannes 100, Monaco 101
Nice 102, Nîmes 103

Fold-out map

Haute-Provence
Côte d'Azur

This Way Provence

Sensual Pleasures

The southeast corner of France, between the Rhône and the Italian border, is a region to stimulate the senses. Its colours have inspired generations of artists: the dark greens of the cypresses and silver grey of the olive trees, the yellows of sunflowers, mimosa and broom, the long low dunes of a lavender desert, the russet earth and ochre houses, the ultramarine and turquoise of the Mediterranean. Listen to its sounds—the incessant chirping of crickets, the thud and click of boules in a game of *pétanque* beneath the plane trees, ice cubes tinkling in a glass of *pastis*. Smell the air, filled with the flowery scents of Grasse, wild herbs, sweet onions and garlic. Taste the sun-ripe figs and peaches, melons and apricots; sweet peppers, courgettes and aubergines blending in a spicy *ratatouille*; the fish and saffron *bouillabaisse*; the wines. And feel the warm touch of the sun—and the occasional bite of the mistral wind.

From Province to Provence

In around 600 BC, Greeks from Phocaea, an Ionian city north of present-day Izmir, sailed over the Mediterranean and founded a trading post at Massalia—now Marseille. Theirs was the first influence on this region, which adopted their skills and sea-faring knowledge. Strategically located between Rome and the Iberian peninsula, it later became a Roman province—Provincia Narbonensis—opening up the lands of Gaul, Britain and Germany to the advance of the Roman legions. To this day, you can still see extraordinary buildings from this period. The cultures mingled, leaving a mixed genetic heritage that goes to explain the relaxed attitude of the people and their garrulous charm.

Medieval times were fraught with invasions, wars, massacres and countless bloody assaults in the name of religion. The people barricaded their villages with defensive ramparts, or built them on the heights like eyries, out of sight and out of arrows' reach.

The core of today's Provence is an ancient *comté* or earldom, to which were added the earldoms of Orange, Nice, Tende, the Papal enclave of the Comtat Venaissin around Avignon, and Monaco, still an independent principality. The boundaries of Provence were defined after the French Revolution, and it was divided into five administrative *départements*, namely Vaucluse, Var, Bouches-du-Rhône, Alpes-Maritimes and Alpes de Haute-Provence. Today, with the addition of a sixth *département*, the Hautes-Alpes, the region has 4.5 million inhabitants and an area of 31,400 sq km (12,120 sq miles). Its capital, Marseille, is France's second-largest city, after Paris, and the biggest port in the entire Mediterranean basin.

From Riviera to Côte d'Azur

East of Marseille, the town of Cassis is the official start of the Côte d'Azur or Azure Coast, the French part of the Riviera (from the Italian word for "shore") sweeping all the way to La Spezia. The evocative name Côte d'Azur first appeared in print as the title of a book by Stephen Liégard, printed in 1887, vaunting the charms of this craggy coast "just 13 hours by train from Paris".

Three massifs form its backdrop—la Sainte-Baume, les Maures, l'Esterel. Nearer to the Italian border the mountain peaks crowd ever closer together; this is the tail-end of the Alps, hurtling into the sea. Here and there, the high cliffs are breached by deep rocky inlets, or *calanques*, filled with water of an incredible turquoise blue. Nestling in every bay along the coast is a resort, with beaches of sand in the west, of pebbles in the east. They were "discovered" by English travellers in the mid-18th century, in search of rest and respite from the damp and dreary climate of northern Europe. Before long, splendid hotels and mansions were built in every extravagant style from baroque to Moorish. Everyone who was any-

one, European royalty, Russian aristocracy, high society and hangers-on, flocked to the sunny, sheltered stretch of coast between Cannes and Menton, where they spent their days walking up and down the sea-front promenades beneath the tropical palms, and their nights in the casinos. After the Edwardians and the Victorians, after the Belle Epoque and its princes came the Années Folles—the Thirties, with their cohorts of American movie stars, film directors and millionaires, the Fitzgeralds, Valentino and Gertrude Stein.

The Real Provence

The glamorous Côte d'Azur is just a frill tacked onto the homespun fabric of Provence. Between the barren, windswept reaches of the Maritime Alps forming its eastern boundary and the fertile lowland of the Rhône Valley, the landscape is rugged, even harsh in places, with the limestone hills of the Luberon and Monts de Vaucluse, the rocky summits of the Alpilles, Mont Ventoux and Mont Saint-Victoire. The ruins of ancient castles cling to craggy peaks, above picturesque villages of stone houses packed tightly together, their shutters closed to keep out the sun. Once abandoned because of its aridity, the land is now fertile. Market stalls are heaped high with local produce: luscious fruit and vegetables; green-gold olive oil; glistening olives; black truffles; goat's and ewe's cheeses soft as cream or hard as pebbles; honey from bees that gorge on lavender, thyme and acacia; light and fruity wines. This is a place to savour the simple things in life.

Flashback

In the Beginning

Dwellings found in the caves of Terra Amata near Nice are estimated to be 400,000 years old. The later Cro-Magnon culture has left traces in other caves: the paintings at Morgiou have been dated at around 27,000 BC. Pottery and agriculture began to take form towards 6000 BC. The presence of dolmens shows that the Neolithic culture appeared fairly early in this region. From around 1800 BC people started trading, while Ligurian tribes settled in the hinterland, moving later to the coastal areas. With the arrival of the Iron Age, especially from the beginning of the 4th century BC, they intermingled with Celtic populations coming down from the north. Fortified towns were built on heights, and the land was shared among a confederation of kingdoms inhabited by several different tribes, notably the Celtic Voconces in the Ouvèse valley (near Vaison-la-Romaine), and the Celto-Ligurian Salyes, with their capital at Entremont, north of Marseille.

Greek Colonization

Around 600 BC, Greeks from Phocaea, an Ionian town north of present-day Izmir, founded a trading post at Massalia—the future Marseille. Vines and olives were introduced, and Massalia soon become the economic centre of the region, exporting its wine to Greece. Gradually, economic ties were formed with the Celto-Ligurian settlements of the hinterland. Massalia developed into a city with its own treasury at Delphi. New trading posts were set up at Glanum (not far from Saint-Rémy-de-Provence), Avignon, Cavaillon, Antibes and Nice. Massalia opened up sea routes to West Africa.

The Roman Empire

In 125 BC, fearing the expansion of the Massalians, the Salyes swept over the Greek colonies. The Romans were called in by the Massalians for help, and they immediately seized the opportunity to colonize Provincia Narbonensis. It took them just three years to subdue the region. In 122 BC, the Consul Caius Sextius founded the permanent military encampment of Aquae Sextiae, later to become Aix-en-Provence. Thanks to Julius Caesar's conquest of Gaul, an immense territory was outlined slowly but surely, bounded by the Pyrenees in the west, the Alps to the east, reaching north up to Lake Geneva and taking in the Rhône valley. Veteran soldiers were granted plots of land where their farms gradually developed into colonies, and a road network was laid out. To the east, the Via Julia Augustus, a continuation of the Via Aurelia from Rome, linked Italy to Nice, Antibes, Fréjus, Aix and Nîmes. The Via Agrippa thrust northwards from Arles through Avignon, Orange, Valence and Vienne, opening up the way to Cologne. In the west, the Via Domitia linked Nîmes with today's Languedoc, crossing the Pyrenees into Spain. Gallo-Roman Provence reached its zenith.

The Holy Roman Empire

As Roman power waned, Christianity took root in the south of Gaul. In AD 313, the Christians were granted freedom of worship by Emperor Constantine, who actively promoted their faith. The decline of the Roman Empire paved the way for invasion by Visigoths and Ostrogoths. The Assembly of the Seven Roman Provinces retreated to Arles in 418, and it was the last place to fall to the barbarians, in 476. Within 60 years, the region was shared out like crumbs among various warlords, though it was briefly reunited under the authority of the Frankish kingdom in 536. The region was overrun by Arab armies (eventually defeated by Charles Martel at Poitiers in 732) and increasingly by pirates.

At the end of the 8th century, Charlemagne reigned over all western Europe. In 843 his empire was shared out between his three grandsons; Lothair inherited Italy along with Provence, which was set up as a kingdom. In 933, the kingdom of Arles was created. Uniting Provence and Burgundy, it was at first a nominal dependency of the Holy Roman Empire, then was annexed officially in 1034. However, the counts of Provence retained their autonomy.

All through the 9th and 10th centuries, Saracens raided the coastal areas from their base in the Massif des Maures, until they were finally routed in 972.

Passing from Hand to Hand

Provence was ruled by the Counts of Barcelona in the early 12th century, then by the Counts of Toulouse. The River Rhône, already an important commercial thoroughfare, became a political frontier. In 1246 the earldom of Toulouse came into the hands of the kings of France, while Provence fell to Louis IX's brother Charles I of Anjou, King of Naples and the Two Sicilies. He crushed any signs of independence displayed by the cities.

The region remained in the hands of the Anjou dynasty for 250 years. During this period, the Grimaldis took power over Monaco in 1297; famine and plague swept over the region in 1348; and the earldom of Nice was transferred to the House of Savoy in 1388. In the 15th century, the prosperous reign of Good King René at Aix introduced a rich intellectual and artistic era. Upon his death in 1480, the earldom passed to a nephew who promptly died after bequeathing it to the king of France, Louis XI. In this way, in 1486, the region was joined to the kingdom of France in a union of equals and kept many of its privileges right up to the Revolution.

Papal Lands

Throughout the Middle Ages, there were three large blots on the map of Provence: the independent territories of Orange, Avignon and the Comtat Venaissin. With its capital at Carpentras, the Comtat lay south of the Mont Ventoux and the Barronnies, bounded by the Rhône and the Durance rivers. It became the property of the Holy See in 1274, and when Clement V was elected pope in 1305, he decided to abandon Rome and take up residence here. His predecessor Boniface VIII had been imprisoned for opposing Philippe le Bel (Philip the Fair), king of France, who wanted to assert his independence in face of the Church's temporal power. Jews persecuted in France found refuge in the Comtat, and by 1309 Clement V had set up his court in Avignon. The city was purchased from its legitimate owner, Queen Jeanne, in 1348. Avignon ruled over Christendom for 68 years, and its influence at the time was extraordinary. All succeeding popes were French, and though they did not owe allegiance directly to the king, they were often obliged to submit to his will. In 1377, when Gregory XI returned to Rome at the end of his pontificate, the Great Schism of the West was triggered off, with popes being elected both in Avignon (not recognized) and in Rome. Everything returned to normal in 1449.

Absolute Monarchy

In the early part of the 16th century, Provence was dragged into the conflict opposing François I and Charles V (Holy Roman Emperor and Charles I of Spain) and was invaded in 1524 and in 1536. During the same period, French replaced Provençal as the official administrative language. Scarcely had peace returned when France, and with her Provence, entered the Wars of Religion: Orange and Nîmes adopted the Reformation and the secession of Vaud was beginning to stir. After three decades of terror and destruction, Henri IV signed the Edict of Nantes in 1598, promising freedom of worship.

Under Louis XIV and his heirs, Provence expanded with the incorporation of the Principality of Orange and the earldom of Nice. This was a prelude to conflict with the House of Savoy in 1707, when Provence was invaded, and to the 1746 coalition between Austria and Sardinia, with an offensive that was halted at the gates of Antibes.

The French Revolution

The big cities of Provence—Marseille, Aix and Toulon—went into the Revolution in a bloodbath. Like the rest of the country, the region was split up into *départements*; Avignon and the Comtat Venaissin were joined with France by referendum. Trouble was brewing in Provence, where, with the exception of Marseille, the Royalists had the upper hand. Called in to help, the English took Toulon in 1793, only to be chased out again by the young commander of the siege artillery—Napoleon Bonaparte. Already a General at the age of 26, he launched the Italian campaign from Nice, by then annexed to France, in 1796. On his way back from the Egyptian expedition in 1799, he landed at Saint-Raphaël before returning to Paris. His return visit in 1814 was somewhat less glorious as he left for exile on the island of Elba.

The earldom of Nice was reincorporated into the kingdom of

PIRACY

Pirates attacked and looted the Provençal coast from the early Middle Ages. In the 14th century a warning system was set up: message of attack was passed along a chain of 33 bonfires, and the news could spread from the Camargue to the Maritime Alpes in half an hour! Piracy reached a climax in the 16th century, with sporadic attacks by buccaneers from Genoa and Aragon in the midst of conflict against the Holy Roman Empire; then, despite a nominal alliance with the Sublime Porte (the Ottoman Empire), with recurrent raids by Barbary pirates. Barbarossa, soon seconded by his lieutenants Sinan the Jew and Kemal Reis, seized La Napoule in 1530. Captive crews and local inhabitants were ransomed or sold into slavery on the markets of North Africa. Though naval headquarters were set up at Toulon and coastal fortifications were strengthened, pirates continued their raids until 1802.

Sardinia-Piedmont. When Napoleon escaped from Elba in 1815, he landed at Golfe-Juan with 1500 men and marched up to Paris by the mountainous back-roads of Provene to avoid his Royalist enemies—a route now known as the "Route Napoléon". He entered Paris in triumph, forcing the king to flee to Holland. Over the next 100 days he raised a Grand Army but was defeated by Wellington at Waterloo.

The Rise of the Resorts

At the end of the 18th century, English aristocrats began to spend their winters on the Mediterranean coast. Some of them settled for good. The region enjoyed substantial development, both in Marseille after to the conquest of Algeria in 1830, and in the agricultural regions of Provence, thanks to the construction of canals to help irrigate the fields for market-gardening. Extra impetus was gained by the opening of the Suez Canal in 1869. The earldom of Nice was re-unified definitively with France after a plebiscite held in 1860, extending the border as far as the Alps. The arrival of the railways further helped to develop the region. Luxury hotels and casinos were

built to accommodate and entertain the world's high society. From the queen of England to the tsar of Russia, everyone went south to the French Riviera.

Modern Times

In 1936, the French socialist government granted paid holidays to workers in July or August, and families flocked to the coast. The south of France suffered much hardship between 1939 and 1945. German refugees, artists and writers, settled down or transited through Marseille, and Italian troops occupied Menton in 1940. Two years later, the Free Zone, under the Vichy government, was invaded by the Wehrmacht. The French fleet at Toulon was sunk by the British to keep it out of German hands. While the Italians controlled the Côte d'Azur, the Nazis took the rest of Provence, blowing up Marseille's historic centre in 1943. The Allies landed at Saint-Raphaël and Saint-Tropez on August 15–16, and within two weeks the whole region was liberated. In the 1950s, people started buying cars, the motorways were built, and once again, holidaymakers headed to the Côte d'Azur. Today, tourism is the main source of revenue.

On the Scene

Whether you fly into Nice or Marseille, drive down the motorway and leave it at Orange or Avignon, or take the train to Marseille, your introduction to Provence will be spectacular. The landscape is ever-changing, from the vineyards of the Rhône Valley to the wetlands of the Camargue, from the fields of melon and lavender to the corniche roads between Nice and Menton.

AVIGNON AND REGION

Avignon, Orange, Vaison-la-Romaine, Mont Ventoux, Carpentras, Pernes-les-Fontaines, Fontaine-de-Vaucluse, l'Isle-sur-la-Sorgue, Nîmes, Pont du Gard

Firmly rooted among the vineyards of the Rhône Valley, Avignon and Orange are the northern gateways to Provence. Stretching from these cities to the edge of the Vaucluse plateau is the *département* of Vaucluse, which was a papal state from 1274 until the end of the French Revolution. In the east, heralding the Pré-alpes, is the famous Mont Ventoux, a challenge to participants in the Tour de France cycle race. While you're here it's worth making an excursion west of the Rhône Valley to Nîmes and the Pont du Gard, in the *département* of Languedoc-Roussillon.

The Palace and the Cathedral of the Popes served as a barracks and a prison during the Revolution.

Avignon

During the Bronze Age (2000 BC), dwellings were built on a limestone outcrop high above the Rhône—the beginnings of Avignon. The strategic site of ancient Avenio, translated variously as "river town" or "town of strong wind", was occupied in turn by a Ligurian then a Gaulish *oppidum*, a Roman *castrum* (camp) and citadel, and the town gradually spread down the slopes. Pope Clement V was installed in Avignon in 1390, and it remained the unique and uncontested capital of

Christendom for 68 years. Attracting pilgrims, merchants and artists, it was enhanced with numerous churches and convents. Grandiose palaces and impressive ramparts remain from the time of the popes. A dynamic city on the cultural front, Avignon hosts one of France's most renowned theatre and danse festivals. Museums, 17th- and 18th-century mansions, boutiques, cobbled streets and lively cafés complete the scene.

Ramparts

Built by order of Pope Innocent IV in 1355 to defend the flourishing city, the ramparts completely encircle the historic centre. They were partially restored by Viollet-le-Duc in the 19th century. Some 4.5 km (nearly 3 miles) long, they are punctuated by seven round or square towers and 39 gates—though some of these were added in more recent times to improve the flow of traffic.

Palais des Papes

Pope Benoît XII (1334–42) ordered construction of a residence on the site of a former episcopal palace. Known as the Palais-Vieux (Old Palace), it was modelled on the architecture of the Abbey of Cîteaux and is of rather severe design, with tiny windows and thick walls set around an arcaded courtyard. During his pontificate (1342–52), Benoît's successor Clement VI added two majestic wings and towers over 50 m (164 ft) high, thus creating the Palais-Neuf (New Palace). During the French Revolution, the palace was converted into a barracks, before being restored.

The visit begins in the main courtyard, where pilgrims once gathered to receive the papal blessing and where the International Festival of Avignon has been held every summer since 1947. The Palais-Vieux, set around Benoît XII's cloister, is famed for the superb group of 14th-century frescoes by Simone Martini in the Salle du Consistoire (Consistory Hall), transferred from their original home in the cathedral of Notre-Dame-des-Doms. They bear witness to the emergence of a significant artistic movement reminiscent of the Italian Quattrocento. In the Palais-Neuf, the highlights are the Chambre du Cerf (Stag Chamber) and the Salle de la Grande Audience, with its magnificent fresco of the prophets.

Hôtel des Monnaies

Opposite the palace, the Royal Mint of 1619 today houses the Conservatoire de Musique. It is a remarkable example of baroque architecture, decorated with dragons and eagles copied from the arms of the Borghese family.

Notre Dame-des-Doms

The high square tower of this monumental cathedral looms over the Palais des Papes. Built in the 12th century, it was altered several times, most recently after desecration during the Revolution when it was used as a prison. It is mainly Romanesque but has traces of Gothic frescoes; some of the Avignon popes are entombed in its baroque chapels.

Jardin des Doms

Behind the cathedral, the Garden of the Doms is planted on the summit of a limestone rock 30 m (98 ft) above the Rhône and its plain. It was inhabited from prehistoric times to the Middle Ages. The name may have derived from the installation here of the bishops' residence—*domo episcopali*. When the Palais des Papes was built, the site was left for cattle to graze. In the 18th century it was landscaped as an English park when taking the air became fashionable.

Musée du Petit Palais

Down below, at one end of the Place du Palais, the former archbishops' residence (14th–15th centuries) houses a museum dedicated to medieval and early Renaissance art. Besides the sculpture collection, there are works by Italian painters and artists of the Avignon school.

SUR LE PONT D'AVIGNON...

Everyone knows the words—but no one can say who wrote them. The song was popularized in the middle of the 19th century by the composer Alphonse Adam, for an opera produced in Avignon and called *Le Sourd*, or *l'Auberge Pleine*. Adam is better known as composer of the ballet *Giselle*.

Pont Saint-Bénézet

The famous Pont d'Avignon was named after a shepherd who founded a religious order which collected money for bridge-building. Its aim was to facilitate the pilgrims' way to Santiago de Compostela in Spain. However, when it was constructed, between 1177 and 1185, the Saint-Bénézet bridge was the only one over the lower Rhône, and it enabled the town to develop commercially. After recurrent damage by wars and floods, it was restored several times but abandoned in the 17th century. It stops forlornly in the middle of the river, with only four of its 22 original arches intact, so no one can cross over to Barthelasse island at the other end, where people used to dance in the riverside outdoor cafés that were the inspiration behind the famous song.

The Old Town

From the esplanade of the Palace, you can walk to the spacious Place de l'Horloge at the heart of the old town. On fine days everyone makes a beeline for its shady pavement cafés. Around it are quiet little squares and pedestrian streets lined with boutiques. A flower market is held on Saturdays on Place Crillon.

Wealthy families of the 17th and 18th centuries built opulent town houses here in baroque style. Several are now museums, for instance the Musée Calvet des Beaux-Arts at 65 rue Joseph Vernet, with paintings and sculpture of the 15th–20th centuries, and the Musée Louis Vouland at 17 rue Victor Hugo, devoted to the decorative arts of the 17th and 18th centuries.

Villeneuve-lès-Avignon

Opposite Avignon on the right bank of the Rhône, Villeneuve developed thanks to the Saint-Bénézet bridge, guarded at this end by the Philippe le Bel tower. The pontifical court resided here, and Pope Innocent VI decided to set up the charterhouse of Val-de-Bénédiction. In the 14th century it was the largest in Europe with three cloisters and forty monastic cells. The pope entrusted the decoration of his private chapel to Matteo Giovannetti, whose frescoes can still be admired.

Châteauneuf-du-Pape

Set amidst the vineyards, the village nestles on the sunny slopes of a hill beneath the ruins of the popes' château. Only two majestic sections of a wall remain of the popes' summer residence, built in the 14th century. In the village, you can visit the church of Notre-Dame-de-l'Assomption with fine Romanesque vaulting, and the 10th-century chapel of Saint-Théodoric, which has frescoes in the choir. However, wine is the principal attraction, with tours of the wine cellars and the Musée des Outils de Vigneron du Père Anselme (vineyard tools).

Roquemaure

The relics of Saint Valentine are kept in the collegiate church of Saint-Jean-Baptiste at Roquemaure, on the right bank of the Rhône. Valentine is not only the patron saint of lovers, but also the protector of vines: he saved those of the region from phylloxera in the 19th century. On February 14, the effigy of the saint is carried through the town by inhabitants in fancy dress for the Festa di Poutoun (Kissing Festival).

Orange

The Roman settlement of Arausio was founded in 35 BC by veterans of the 2nd Gallic Legion. The Principality of Orange was inherited by the Flemish family of

The River Rhône dances through the fabled Pont d'Avignon.

Nassau in 1530 and was a refuge for protestants during the Wars of Religion. The city was united with France in 1731. A small modern town sitting in the centre of the Côtes-du-Rhône region, it has preserved two Roman monuments which are listed by UNESCO as World Heritage Sites.

Arc de Triomphe

The triumphal arch that spanned the main street, or *cardo*, of the Roman city was completed around AD 20. It was initially dedicated to the colony, then to the Emperor Tiberius, and the two inscriptions remain. With three arches and two upper storeys, it stands almost 20 m (65 ft) high. Used as a defensive post in the Middle Ages, the arch was actually converted into apartments for the Prince of Orange in the 16th century—all traces of which have now disappeared. Reliefs on both sides of the main gate depict military themes commemorating the Pax Romana.

Roman theatre

Built into the hill of Saint-Eutrope, the theatre is one of the best preserved of the Roman world. It dates from the end of the reign of Emperor Augustus (AD 10–25). The stage wall, 103 m (338 ft) high and 37 m (121 ft) long, is still intact. Originally it was richly decorated, and you can still see fragments of columns, together with a restored statue of Augustus, 3.5 m (11.5 ft) tall. A festival of dramatic and lyrical arts, the Chorégies, was begun in 1860 and is still going strong; 9,000 spectators at a time can enjoy the splendid acoustics.

Musée municipal

Opposite the theatre entrance, the museum occupies a 17th-century town house. It has a small archaeological collection and furniture illustrating the town's history.

Colline de Saint-Eutrope

Behind the theatre, steps lead up to a wooded park on Saint-Eutrope hill and the ruined castle of the Princes of Orange-Nassau. It was destroyed in 1673 by order of Louis XIV. Landmarks are pointed out on a *table d'orientation,* from where there's a wonderful view over the town.

Vaison-la-Romaine

The town is built on several hills. On one side of the Ouvèze River, where the Voconces had their seat, looms the ruined fort of the counts of Toulouse; on the opposite bank, the heights of Puymin and La Villasse were part of the Roman settlement of Vasio Vocontiorum in the 1st century BC. It was an important political and economic centre, and today its remains form the largest archaeological site in France.

Ancient Vaison

In the north sector of the ancient Gallo-Roman city, Puymin hill is entirely devoted to archaeological remains. The theatre could seat up to 5000 spectators; you can also see the thermal baths and several villas. Excavated finds, including a fine mosaic from the Villa des Paons (Peacock Villa) are displayed in the Musée Théo-Desplans in the middle of the complex. The site of La Villasse is lower down, on the other side of Avenue du Général-de-Gaulle.

Lower Town

Marking the boundary of the Villasse site, Rue Trogue-Pompée leads to the Romanesque cathedral of Notre-Dame-de-Nazareth. Built in the 11th century using stone from the Roman buildings and renovated in the following century, it backs onto the Canon's Cloister, which is surrounded by narrow arcades of double columns. Further north, the chapel of Saint-Quenin, with an unusual triangular apse, is supported by Corinthian columns.

Upper Town

A Roman bridge, 17 m (56 ft) long, spans the river Ouvèze with a single arch at the point where the river narrows. In the 12th century, the inhabitants of Vaison, fleeing the insecurity of the lower town, crossed over and settled on the rocky spur of the ancient *oppidum*, where they stayed for 100 years. At the foot of the fortress is a labyrinth of narrow lanes called *calades*. Houses built of stone are squeezed into the double curtain wall of the old ramparts. Today, a number of artisans have infused new life into this district.

Mont Ventoux

Rising to an altitude of 1,909 m (6,263 ft), Mont Ventoux with its white limestone cap reigns over Provence (its name came not from the wind but from Vintur, a god of the summits). A classic stage of the Tour de France cycle race, the mountain is also popular with hikers. With abundant flora, both Mediterranean and Alpine, larch and pine forest and unobtrusive fauna, it is designated as a Biosphere Reserve by UNESCO. The road from Malaucène takes you up to the Tempêtes pass, at an altitude of 1,841 m (6,040 ft), and from there it's easy to reach the top. The view from on high sweeps from the Mediterranean to the Alps.

Sault

This is the start of the "lavender route", where the fields of billowing purple stretch as far as the eye can see—but only in summer. The flowers are harvested from end July to end August, when distillery tours are organized. The glorious lavender festival is celebrated on August 15.

To the west, the deep gorges of the Nesque, popular with hikers, cut deep gashes in the southern flank of Mont Ventoux.

Carpentras

A Celto-Ligurian market town colonized by the Romans, Carpentras took on a certain importance in the 14th century when the popes made it the capital of the Comtat Venaissin. Nowadays a town of 30,000 inhabitants, it has two markets—fruit and vegetables on Fridays and truffles from November to March. The town's other specialities are *berlingots* (white-striped fruit or mint-flavoured boiled sweets) and *fruits confits*: candied fruit. The markets are held beneath the planes of the Allée des Platanes. From here you can see the Italianate façade of the 18th-century Hôtel-Dieu (general hospital). Inside is a 17th-century apothecary's shop.

Following traffic-free Rue de la République to the town centre, you'll arrive at the southern-Gothic Cathédrale Saint-Siffrein, which was begun in 1404 and took 115 years to complete. The

At Pernes-les-Fontaines, the bridge over the Nesque.

cupola over the choir belonged to the original, Romanesque building. On the south side, look for the Jewish door in Flamboyant Gothic style, surmounted by a strange scuplted ball squirming with rodents, the *boule aux rats*. Next to the cathedral, a plain arch dating from the 1st century is the only monument remaining from Roman times; it was built on the ancient forum.

The 14th-century synagogue on Place de la Mairie, reconstructed several times, dates back to the time when the Jews of the South of France were persecuted by Philippe le Bel and took refuge in the Comtat Venaissin.

North of the centre, the Porte d'Orange is all that is left of the second medieval town wall, built at the end of the 14th century. It is topped by a tower affording a fine view over the banks of the Auzon river.

Pernes-les-Fontaines

Capital of the Comtat Venaissin from the 10th century to the beginning of the 14th, famous for its 37 fountains, the town lies at the western end of the Vaucluse plateau on the banks of the river Nesque. Parts of the 14th–15th century ramparts are still standing, with three gates and several town houses. The Vichet House is the only factory in France making communion wafers. Nearby, the 12th-century Tour Ferrande has some 13th-century frescoes, and you can see local traditional costumes in the Musée du Costume Comtadin. Further east is the Tour de l'Horloge, once the castle keep.

The Porte Notre-Dame (1548), down below, leads from the Place du Cormoran to a charming bridge over the Nesque; on one of its piers is the chapel of Notre-Dame-des-Graces. Cross over to the other bank to see the 11th-century Romanesque church of Notre-Dame-de-Nazareth.

Fontaine-de-Vaucluse

Here in the narrow Vallis Clausa, the closed valley that gave its name to Vaucluse, is the source of the Sorgue river. It springs from a bottomless sinkhole linked to a huge subterranean network that collects the waters from the Vaucluse plateau. Although the flow sometimes dries up in summer, it can rise to 200 cu m (7000 cu ft) per second in spring.

The enchanting setting (described by Petrarch in his sonnets) is riddled with grottoes and chasms. They were explored by the speleologist Norbert Casteret, who put together the impressive collection of stalagmites and stalactites displayed in the Monde souterrain. Also on the bank of the Sorgue is the Vallis Clausa paper mill, which can be visited, together with a glassworks and the evocative Musée de la Résistance. In the village, a house has been converted into the Musée Pétrarque (the 14th-century Italian poet studied in Avignon and stayed a while here).

L'Isle-sur-la-Sorgue

This charming town spreads over several islands formed by five branches of the Sorgue snaking around and through it. With its canals and moss-grown waterwheels, it is inevitably called the Venice of Provence. In summer, a market is held on the water, and nautical jousting is organized. The Sunday morning market is well known in the antique-dealing world, and even during the week the streets are lined with shops selling all manner of desirable antiques and appealing bric-à-brac *(brocante).*

If you manage to find a parking space, stroll around town to admire the handsome Renaissance houses, the church of Notre-Dame-des-Anges (with a baroque interior dating from the end of the 17th century), and the apothecary's shop of the Hôtel-Dieu.

Nîmes

This city, supposedly founded by the god Nemausus around a spring that wells up at the foot of

Mont Cavalier, became one of the most illustrious of Roman Gaul after it had been beautified by Emperor Augustus. In a pivotal position between Provence and Languedoc (to which it belongs) and on the main route to Spain, it still boasts monuments from this glorious period. Its coat of arms features a crocodile chained to a palm tree, the emblem of the first colonists who were veterans of the Roman legions in Egypt. Annexed to the earldom of Toulouse in 1185, then to France in 1229, Nîmes was a Protestant haven during the Wars of Religion. Today it has 135,000 inhabitants. Most of the monuments and sites of interest are contained within a triangle in the town centre, bordered by three boulevards, Victor-Hugo to the west, Gambetta to the north and Admiral-Courbet to the east.

Maison Carrée

Built around AD 5 and known simply as the Square House, a monumental temple fronted by a colonnade stands on the Roman forum, to the northwest of the town centre. Raised on a podium that emphasizes its majesty, the temple has been miraculously preserved in its entirety. It was dedicated to the Imperial cult of Caius and Lucius Caesar, the grandsons of Augustus. In the 16th century it was converted into private apartments and was even used as stables. Since then it has been restored, and inside you can see an exhibition detailing the building's history and architecture.

Opposite, the modern Carré d'Art was designed by Norman Foster and inspired by the temple's four-square shape. It houses a multi-media centre and a museum of contemporary art.

Amphitheatre

The magnificent amphitheatre, built between AD 90 and 100, is one of the best preserved in the Roman world. Its efficient system of galleries, both concentric and radiating out from the centre, provides rapid access to the tiers of seats, where there's enough room for 23,000 spectators. Over the years, people built houses inside the walls, and at the beginning of the 19th century, there were still 700 people living there. Nowadays, the arena is again used for sporting activities, though bullfights and traditional bull-running have replaced the gladiatorial combats of Roman times.

From October to April, the arena is covered and tennis tournaments and ice-skating shows are held there.

Historic Centre

On the quaint Place du Marché, surrounded by sunny café terraces, you can see a "crocodile fountain" and palm tree that echo the design of the town's coat of arms.

Explore the narrow side streets to discover handsome *hôtels particuliers* and attractive old houses such as the 12th-century Maison Romane, decorated with friezes, on the corner of Rue de la Madeleine and Place aux Herbes. This square has many inviting outdoor cafés, where you can sit and admire the unusual cathedral of Saint Castor, in Romanesque-Byzantine style.

On Boulevard Amiral-Courbet, the Gate of Augustus (16 BC) is one of only two surviving from the original walls. These were 6 km (4 miles) long with a dozen gates and around 80 towers.

Museums

The Musée d'Archéologie has some splendid items from the Roman era. The Musée du Vieux Nîmes recounts the city's history, and south of the town centre, the Musée des Beaux-Arts is known for its lovely Roman mosaic depicting the *Wedding of Admetus*.

Jardins de la Fontaine

Reached by way of the Quai de la Fontaine alongside the canal, this tranquil wooded park was laid out in the 18th century on the southern slope of Mont Cavalier. At the foot of the hill is the spring that gave rise to the Nemausus of antiquity. A shrine was built here during the reign of Augustus, at the end of the 1st century BC. You can see the remains of a structure known as the Temple of Diana, although its exact purpose is unknown. Right at the top, the Tour Magne, at 32 m (105 ft) the tallest tower on the Roman wall, looms over the town.

Pont du Gard

In order to supply Nîmes with water in the 1st century AD, the Romans undertook the construction of an amazing aqueduct 50 km (31 miles) long. Striding over valleys and moorland, it was designed to carry 20,000 cu m (700,000 cu ft) of water per day into the town from a spring near Uzès. To span the wide Gorges du Gardon, the engineers designed a bridge of exceptional dimensions, 275 m (900 ft) long and 48 m (157 ft) high, supported by three levels of arches. Listed as a World Heritage Site by UNESCO, the Pont du Gard is a work of exceptional beauty in a wild and grandiose natural setting, and an outstanding architectural achievement.

If you get this far, it's well worth continuing a little further to the well-preserved medieval town of Uzès, used as an authentic-looking film set for *The Three Musketeers*.

ALPILLES, LUBERON AND HAUTE-PROVENCE

Saint-Rémy-de-Provence, Les Baux-de-Provence, Tarascon, Petit Luberon, Gordes, Pays des Ocres, Haute-Provence

The *département* of Vaucluse opens onto limestone mountains to the south and east; it shares the Alpilles chain with neighbouring Bouches-du-Rhône, while the Luberon stretches eastward, a succession of wooded hills and meadows, vineyards and olive plantations. Further east again, Haute-Provence is wilder and windier, a foretaste of the Alps.

Saint-Rémy-de-Provence

The most important town of the Alpilles, Saint-Rémy is descended from the Glanum of antiquity. The physician and astrologer Nostradamus was born here in 1503, but it is better known today thanks to Vincent Van Gogh, who spent many months here and painted some of his most famous works. Visitors from the world over stroll through the picturesque old town, exploring its alleys and squares, admiring its fountains, sitting in the plane-shaded courtyards and in the outdoor cafés. The Tourist Office organizes guided tours around Van Gogh's favourite haunts.

Erosion has sculpted red ochre needles at Roussillon.

Old Town

On the south side of town, Porte Saint-Paul opens onto the narrow streets of the historic centre. Follow Rue Hoche, a string of houses built on the old ramparts, to no. 6, the birthplace of Nostradamus.

The collegiate church of Saint-Martin with its huge neoclassical porch and great baroque organ was built between 1821 and 1825, after the original Romanesque church collapsed one night: only its 14th-century bell tower was left standing.

On Place Favier, shaded by chestnut trees, is the Mistral de Montdragon, a mansion housing the Musée des Alpilles, with displays of geology, history, art and popular traditions.

The nearby Musée archéologique on Rue du Parage has been set up inside the Hôtel de Sade, built in the 15th century on the ruins of Roman baths. The history of ancient Glanum is related through sculpture and ordinary household objects. Further east near the Mairie (town hall), the Centre d'Art Présence Van Gogh (8 rue Estrine) holds temporary exhibitions and pays tribute to the great artist with photographs of his paintings.

Saint-Paul-de-Mausole

At the southern exit from town, next to the site of Glanum, this former monastery is a fine example of Provençal Romanesque architecture. It owes its fame to the year-long stay that Van Gogh made here from May 1889 to May 1890, after he had sliced off his ear in Arles. The place is still a psychiatric institution, but it is open to visitors who can see the painter's room, restored exactly as Vincent described it to his brother. Coming back to his senses here, Van Gogh painted more than 150 canvases, which count among his most important works (*The Irises*, *The Starry Night*, and so on). The monastery has a gardened cloister with finely sculpted capitals.

Glanum

Collectively known as Les Antiques, the Mausoleum of the Julii (a great Roman family) dating from 30–20 BC and a Roman triumphal arch built in 20 AD stand beside the road at the exit of a narrow valley commanded by the peaks of the Alpilles. Both structures are decorated with carved reliefs. Until 1921, they were the only visible signs of the city of Glanum, which was in fact only a short distance away, concealed by soil deposits and olive plantations. Excavation revealed other finds, indicating that the site was Celto-Ligurian, founded in the 6th century BC through the influence of the Greeks of Marseille. The city underwent a great expansion in the 2nd century BC just before the Romans arrived. They added a forum, temples, baths, houses and a surrounding wall. However, the ruins are difficult to decipher, except by expert eyes, apart from a reconstructed section of the temple of Glanum.

Les Baux-de-Provence

High above the plain, the ancient limestone hills of the Alpilles break up into a multitude of rocky spurs. One of them stretches out like a great headland between two valleys, the Val d'Enfer and the Vallon de la Fontaine. This lofty site was chosen for construction of a citadel in the Middle Ages. After the 10th century, the history of Les Baux is entwined with that of its feudal lords, valiant crusaders who claimed to be descendants of Balthazar, one of the three Wise Men. They always reigned supreme, refusing to acknowledge the sovereignty of the counts of Barcelona or the kings of France. At the height of their glory they ruled over all the Alpilles and as far as the Crau plain. Les Baux became a barony and flourished even more during the Renaissance when the castle was expanded. A large Protestant community settled here, but in

1632 Cardinal Richelieu ordered the destruction of the fortress—and the inhabitants were made to pay the costs.

Raised to the status of a marquisate, Les Baux was given to the Grimaldis until 1791 when it was annexed to France. The site was deserted and it sank into oblivion. Today it is beseiged by hordes of tourists in summer.

The Village

Rue Porte Mage leads you into the cluster of medieval and Renaissance stone houses, most of them occupied by boutiques and restaurants. The Manville mansion, built in 1571 around a porticoed courtyard, is now the town hall. Exhibitions of contemporary art are held there. Down below on Place Louis-Jou, clinging to the ramparts and watching over the Vallon de la Fontaine, is the Musée des Santons—miniature Nativity figurines, the oldest dating from the 18th century. The Eyguières Gate was the only way into the village until 1866. Rue de la Calade climbs up to Place François-de-Hérain, where the delightful late-16th century Hôtel des Porcelets is home to the Musée Yves-Brayer. This figurative painter (1907–90) found his inspiration in Mediterranean subjects.

Outside the church of Saint-Vincent is a small dome-topped turret decorated with a gargoyle: it was a sort of lantern that was lit up whenever one of the villagers died. The church has three wide naves; the one on the right-hand side is Carolingian, dating from the 10th century. The central nave, 12th-century, is Romanesque, and the left-hand one is from the 15th century. Opposite the church, the 17th-century Chapelle des Pénitents is decorated with large frescoes depicting the shepherds of the Nativity, by Yves Brayer.

The Castle

Rue du Château leads up to the entrance of the fortress, languishing on the heights above the village. All that is left is a pile of romantic ruins studded by the Sarrasine and Paravelle towers, a keep, and the remains of chapels and houses, some of them hollowed out of the rock. Pick up an audioguide at the entrance; it's the best way of making sense of the scattered stones.

From the edge of the cliff, the view takes in all of the Alpilles. You can see several models of medieval war machines.

Cathédrale d'Images

Val d'Enfer, literally Hell Valley, takes its name from a sombre medieval tale relating that Viscount Raymond Turenne, turned brigand, used to throw his hostages down here if ransom was refused. In one of the many disused chalk quarries, the Cathédrale d'Images presents a stunning 30-minute audiovisual show in which thousands of photographs on a given theme are continuously projected onto the white walls that form a giant screen.

Fontvieille

West of Baux, and after Maussane-les-Alpilles, Fontvieille is France's leading producer of olive oil. It celebrates the memory of Alphonse Daudet, author of *Lettres de mon Moulin (Letters from my Mill)* written in 1866. Dedicated readers can follow the Daudet trail, starting from the mill of Saint Pierre, on top of a hill dominating the town, to the château of Montauban, where the writer stayed on several occasions and which now houses an exhibition on his works.

Tarascon

This is another name familiar to readers of Alphonse Daudet. Home town of Tartarin de Tarascon, the town on the banks of the Rhône has dedicated a museum (55 boulevard Itam) to the colourful character. Tarascon is also the town of the Tarasque, a legendary bloodthirsty monster that lived below ground and preyed on the population until being finally vanquished by Saint Martha. In the 12th-century royal collegiate church, a large, brightly painted wooden Tarasque sits biding his time all year round, disturbed only in June when the inhabitants commemorate his demise. The church has been much restored; it has a Romanesque doorway and houses the relics of Saint Martha. In the crypt there is a 3rd-century sarcophagus. In the Chapelle Sainte-Marthe is a brass replica of the golden reliquary donated by Louis XI in 1470—the original weighed 30 kg!

The Fortress

Standing guard over the collegiate church and the Rhône, this moated castle with high battlemented towers was built in 1400 by Louis II, Duke of Anjou and Count of Provence. His second son, known as the Good King René, converted it into a Renaissance palace. The majority of its stately rooms with their grand fireplaces have painted and coffered ceilings. Some have vaulting, with carvings of human and mythical figures at the base. There is a magnificent group of 17th-century Flemish tapestries, the *Tenture de l'Histoire de Scipion l'Africain* relating the story of Scipio Africanus, as well as an apothecary's shop. The view from the terrace sweeps over the town and river.

Petit Luberon

On the right bank of the River Durance, east of the Alpilles, Cavaillon is the French melon capital and gateway to the Petit Luberon with its fields of fruit and vegetables, orchards, vines, *garrigue* and high wooded hills rising to 700 m (2,300 ft). The hills, between here and the Monts de Vaucluse, are topped by a host of villages each as charming as their names—Ménerbes, Bonnieux, Lourmarin, Cucuron.... Many were abandoned and the stone houses left to disintegrate until the 1970s when artists and craftsmen found there the peace and quiet they were yearning for. This region, and beyond to Gordes, Apt and Roussillon, lies within the great natural regional park of the Luberon. It is Peter Mayle country, featured in his books *A Year in Provence* and *Toujours Provence*.

Oppède-le-Vieux

The quiet town of Oppède sits on the northern flank of a rocky spur. It is one of the prettiest villages of the Luberon, and has been partially restored by artists. On the heights are ruined mansions torn apart by tree roots, along with the 12th-century church of Notre-Dame-d'Alidon, and just above them the vestiges of a castle overgrown by vegetation. There's a fabulous view over the olive groves of the plain on one side and the cedar-planted valley on the other.

Ménerbes

Peter Mayle's adopted village hunkers down over a long promontory, like a great ship sailing over an ocean of olive trees. Wander around the narrow streets where cats slink round the corners and wisteria clings to the ancient stone walls. In the middle, surrounded by a ring of sturdy houses with heavy doors, stands the feudal castle, built in the 13th century (it's privately owned). You can visit the 14th-century church and look around the Musée du Tire-Bouchon, exhibiting more than 1000 corkscrews from the 17th century to the present.

Lacoste

Facing its rival Bonnieux on another hilltop, the hamlet of Lacoste is a tranquil place, oozing charm. It boasts an 11th-century castle, now in ruins, but which belonged to the grandfather of the Marquis de Sade. Condemned in Paris for his scandalous prose and libertine manners, the sadistic marquis fled here in 1771.

Bonnieux

Wrapped around a peak dominating the Calavon plain, the village huddles behind the shelter of its

The houses of Gordes packed closely together on a hilltop.

ramparts. It was once a pontifical city. Narrow streets and stairways climb to the summit, crowned by the upper town church at the top of a flight of 86 steps. Encircled by cedars and yews, it stands aloof, affording a splendid panorama over the surrounding landscape. South of the village is the Musée de la Boulangerie, a small bakery museum.

Higher up, in the foothills of the Luberon, you enter a forest of Atlas cedars. If you go north to Roussillon from here, stop to see the Pont Julien (Julian Bridge), built by the Romans to ford the Calavon River at the end of the 1st century BC.

Lourmarin

Officially awarded the title of one of the most beautiful villages in France, Lourmarin, at the head of a dale forming the natural boundary between the Petit and the Grand Luberon, has bewitched many an artist and writer. Albert Camus, author of *La Peste,* is buried in the local cemetery. A short distance out of the village, the elegant castle was begun in the 12th century but dates mostly from the 15th and 16th centuries and has two distinct parts, Château-Vieux and the Renaissance Château-Neuf. It is the property of the Aix-en-Provence Academy of Arts, Science and

Literature and is host to artists and researchers all year round. You can visit the interior and see the monumental spiral staircase.

Silvacane

In the south of the Parc du Luberon on the left bank of the Durance, the Romanesque Abbey of Silvacane is a huge 12th-century monastic ensemble, with church, cloister, refectory, dormitory, chapter house and library. Along with its sister houses of Thoronet and Sénanque, equally sober but rather better preserved, it bears witness to the widespread influence of the Cistercian Order in the Middle Ages.

Gordes

Tightly gripping the southern slope of a hillock in the Monts de Vaucluse, Gordes delights in a spectacular site that dominates the Luberon from afar. The 11th-century stronghold, remodelled in Renaissance style in the 16th century, guards a labyrinth of winding streets teeming with art galleries and stylish boutiques. The 12th-century Romanesque church was once a stage on the pilgrims' route to Santiago de Compostella.

Outside the village, the *village des bories* is a group of well-preserved dry-stone beehive-shaped dwellings recalling the hard life of the Luberon peasants in the 19th century.

Sénanque

A minor road through the whispering olive groves leads to the Cistercian Abbey of Sénanque, a jewel of Provençal Romanesque art. Founded in the 12th century in a forsaken valley today planted with lavender, the abbey took some 100 years to build. Since 1988, it has been returned to a community of monks who harvest the lavender. Like all the houses of the order, dormitory, abbey church, cloister and rooms are of grandiose austerity. There is an excellent bookshop. If you are lucky, your guide may give an impromptu rendering of Gregorian chant in the church choir.

Pays des Ocres

East of Gordes, between the Plateau de Vaucluse and the Montagne du Luberon, is a fertile region of orchards and lavender fields, also reputed for its ochre quarries. These seams of yellow pigment are silica deposits between the limestone mountain ranges. They are the largest in the world and were discovered in 1780. The ochre was soon exploited and exported all over the world. The industry was abandoned after World War I and the walls of the quarries, eroded by rain, wind and frost, were gradually transformed into a fantastic landscape of peaks, ridges and needles, burnt red by the sun.

Apt

Apt makes candied fruit, which sits in tantalizing rows of glistening, bejewelled colours in the confectioners' windows. It is made from all kinds of whole fruit from cherries to melons. Apt makes an excellent base for exploring the Luberon, or for doing your shopping if you're staying out in a village. The Saturday market is known far and wide.

A stroll through the centre will take you past the ruined ramparts, an archaeological museum and the cathedral of Sainte-Anne, founded in the 12th century, which houses supposed relics of the mother of the Virgin Mary.

At the Maison du Luberon on Place Jean-Jaurès, you will find all necessary information on walking or cycling trips in the area, on the flora and fauna of the national park, as well as a palaeontological museum.

Colorado

A 15-minute drive east of Apt, near the village of Rustrel, the area signposted as "Colorado" has red and orange rock formations reminiscent of the canyons of the American west. From the car park, several footpaths *(sentiers)* are marked through the old iron and ochre quarries. The Sentier du Sahara and slightly shorter Sentier des Cheminées de Fées (fairy chimneys), with its famous rock called the Demoiselle Coiffée (young lady with hat), are the most spectacular.

Roussillon

West of Apt, this adorable village with its ochre houses, sloping streets and tiny paved squares, is an ideal spot to linger at a sunny pavement café. A short climb up a street spanned by the belfry tower will bring you to the church and the ancient *castrum*. From there you can see the jagged cliffsides of the old quarries. The Sentier de l'Ocre trails round their base, and discloses a view of the fantastic Cirque des Aiguilles.

As you leave the village by the Apt road, look out for the Conservatoire des Ocres, on the site of an old factory that closed down in 1964. It has taken on the mission of preserving the knowledge of the old ochre workers. Guided tours recount the processes involved.

Haute-Provence

When you leave the sheltered fruit-growing region of the Durance valley, you'll notice that the landscape becomes wilder, colder and rockier.

Manosque

The gateway to Haute-Provence is a charming little town ringed by boulevards built on the site of the old ramparts. Manosque is particularly associated with the memory of the writer Jean Giono. A plaque at 14 rue Grande marks his childhood home.

Rue Grande opens onto the vast Place de l'Hôtel de Ville and the church of Notre-Dame-du-Romigier. The lower parts have kept their original 11th-century Romanesque style. The altar is composed of a 5th-century early-Christian sarcophagus in Carrara marble. There is also a greatly revered wooden Black Madonna, dating from the 11th century. Your walk through the old town ends at the 14th-century Soubeyron Gate.

Opposite the Saunerie Gate at 1 boulevard Elémir-Bourges, the Centre Jean-Giono is dedicated to the writer and his works. At no. 9, the Fondation Carzou (open Fridays to Sundays) exhibits a huge painting of the *Apocalypse*.

To round off your visit to Manosque, walk up to the top of Mont d'Or, where there are the ruins of a castle of the counts of Toulouse and a view of the town, the river Durance and the Alps.

Forcalquier

Capital of an independent state in the Middle Ages, Forcalquier stands on a promontory between the Lure mountain and the Haut Luberon. On Mondays a big market takes place at the foot of the Romanesque and Gothic co-cathedral of Notre-Dame-du-Bourguet; it is one of the rare places where you can still buy a genuine Basque beret.

The 13th-14th century Couvent des Cordeliers is open for visits but only on Tuesdays and Thursdays.

Near Mane, 3 km (2 miles) south, the Salagon Priory has a lovely 12th-century Romanesque

OCHRE

When it is mined from the quarries, raw ochre, naturally yellow in colour, consists of 80–90% sand and 10–20% pigment. In order to recuperate the pigments, the sand has to be separated off by washing and decanting. In the old days, the ochre paste was collected in basins where it dried in the sun. Cut into bricks of 22 kg to simplify handling, it was then baked for between 15 and 32 hours, a process that resulted in a larger range of colours, according to the length of the baking. The foreman could judge the baking time by smell! The ochre was then reduced to powder in a mill. It was mainly exported to rubber-producing countries, where it was used as a dye in the manufacture of rubber.

church and a Renaissance priory. You can look around the botanical gardens tended by the Musée conservatoire ethnologique.

Ganagobie

Northeast of Forcalquier, beyond the village of Lurs, the Benedictine priory of Ganagobie stands on a solitary wooded spur looking out over the Durance. This masterpiece of 10th-century Romanesque architecture is famous for the carved portal of the church and its 12th-century mosaic paving. As a community of monks lives in the monastery, only part of it is open for visits, from 3 to 5 p.m.

Moustiers-Sainte-Marie

At the northern end of Sainte-Croix lake, gateway to the Verdon Gorges, this village of 600 inhabitants nestles at the foot of a cliff straddling a torrent. In the 18th century, it was an important ceramics *(faïence)* centre, a tradition that is still maintained in many workshops and recounted in a museum. The Romanesque church of Notre-Dame-de-Beauvoir (12th century) used to be known for its bell tower that trembled in time with the bells. From here, climb the series of stairways that lead up to the chapel of Notre-Dame, miraculously poised in a notch in the cliffs, between two high rocks. High above, the rocks are linked by a chain, 225 m (738 ft) long, set with a star. It is said to symbolize the adventure of a crusader who returned safe and sound from captivity by the Saracens—

JEAN GIONO

Born in Manosque on March 30, 1895, Giono was the son of a cobbler with Piedmontese origins, and a mother who took in ironing. Through his novels he became the voice of Haute-Provence and its history. He started out as a bank clerk, but the publication of *Colline* (translated as *Hill of Destiny*) in 1928 and *Un de Baumugnes* (tr. *Lovers are Never Losers*) in 1929 were such a success he was able to devote himself entirely to literature. He bought a villa, Lou Paraïs, above the village (visits by appointment on Fridays), where he lived till the end of his days. His novels, initially about living in harmony with the land and a quest for the simple life, later developed into the search for a universal philosophy—*Le Hussard sur le Toit* (1951, tr. *The Horseman on the Roof*), *Le Bonheur Fou* (1957, tr. *The Straw Man*), for example. Elected to the Académie Goncourt in 1954, Giono died in Manosque in 1970.

at least, that's the story as related by the Provençal poet Frédéric Mistral.

Gorges du Verdon

Rising in the Alps, the fast-flowing river has carved out, over 20 km (12 miles), the longest canyon in Europe. It's also the deepest, at 700 m (2300 ft). Winding roads on each side of the gorge, punctuated by viewpoints, run breathtakingly close to the edge. The southern road is called the Corniche Sublime, and boasts the Mescla "balcony", the Cavaliers and Baucher cliffs, and the Cirque de Vaumale. The Route des Crêtes on the north side of the gorge loops around from the village of Palud-sur-Verdon. From Point Sublime, below Rougon village, you get one of the best views over a bend in the river.

If you want to hike around the gorge, take the Martel trail (GR4) from the Chalet de la Maline to Point Sublime, a distance of 14 km (9 miles). The lower reaches of the Verdon are calmer, and you can go kayaking, rafting or canyoning. You can swim in Sainte-Croix lake, downstream. The villages on the shore are deserted in winter but turn into mini resorts in fine weather.

Bird's-eye view of the meandering Verdon from Point Sublime.

Arles
Pâques
2001
La Feria du 13 au 16 Avril
Vendredi 13 Avril
11 H
NOVILLADA sans Picadors
6 Christophe FANO 6
de MIRAMAS
JONATHAN VEYRUNES
JEREMY BANTI
CURRO REYES
F. JAVIER
GARCIA LANGA
JULIEN PICCINI
17 H
CORRIDA DE TOROS
6 VICTORIANO DEL RIO 6
de MADRID
ENRIQUE PONCE
EL JULI
JUAN BAUTISTA
Samedi 14 Avril
11 H
NOVILLADA Piquée
6 SAN MARTIN 6
de CACERES
CESAR JIMENEZ
YVAN GARCIA
JULIEN MILETTO
17 H
CORRIDA DE TOROS
6 ALCURRUCEN 6
de BADAJOZ
Victor PUERTO
EL CALIFA
SÉBASTIEN CASTELLA
Dimanche 15 Avril
11 H
CORRIDA DE TOROS
6 PARTIDO DE RESINA 6
de SEVILLE
FERNANDEZ MECA
JUAN JOSE PADILLA
ANTONIO FERRERA
17 H
CORRIDA DE TOROS
6 BALTASAR IBAN 6
de MADRID
JUAN MORA
DAVILLA-MIURA
ANTONIO LOSADA
Lundi 16 Avril
11 H
CORRIDA DE REJON
6 LOS ESPARTALES 6
de BADAJOZ
MANO A MANO
JOAO MOURA
ANDY CARTAGENA
17 H
CORRIDA DE TOROS
6 EL PILAR 6
de SALAMANCA
FINITO DE CORDOBA
MANUEL CABALLERO
JUAN BAUTISTA

CAMARGUE

Arles, Saint-Gilles, Camargue Regional Natural Park, Saintes-Maries-de-la-Mer, Aigues-Mortes

Shortly before it reaches the Mediterranean, the Rhône splits into two branches: the Petit Rhône to the west and the Grand Rhône to the east, flowing to the edge of the Plaine de la Crau. They outline a triangle of lush swampland—the Grande Camargue of salt marsh and ricefields, covering some 750 sq km (290 sq miles). West of the Petit Rhône in the direction of Aigues-Mortes, the Petite Camargue forms a sort of island. Grande and Petite Camargue together comprise a regional natural park, and with the addition of the nature reserve around the Etang de Vaccarès, are home to a huge flock of pink flamingos, as well as a stopover for thousands of migratory birds. This is also the land of bulls and horses, and the men that herd them, *manadiers* and *gardians*.

Arles

Set a rocky promontory beside the Rhône, Arles is a city apart. The "little Rome of the Gauls" still boasts imposing monuments from its first golden age, introduced by Julius Caesar and the veterans of his 6th legion in 46 BC. The last outpost of Roman Gaul, the city lost its prestige when it fell into the hands of the Visigoths in 476, only to be resuscitated in the Middle Ages. The town centre lies between the Rhône to the north and the Boulevard des Lices to the south, hemmed by busy street cafés. It's here, near the arena, that the Saturday market is held, and where the bulls are released into the streets at fiesta time. All Camargue pours into Arles for these events, the *gardians* astride their proud white horses.

Bullfighters and herdsmen compete during the ferias.

Amphitheatre

Almost 2000 years old, the amphitheatre is in an excellent state of preservation. It is 136 m (149 yd) long and 107 m (117 yd) wide, with seating in elliptical galleries. In the Middle Ages it was topped with towers and converted into a fortress, and ended up being filled with dwellings. In the 1820s there were still 212 houses and two churches within its walls. A few years later they were all razed, and the capture of Algiers was celebrated by a bull race in the arena. Since then the corridas of the two Arles ferias have always been held here.

Roman Theatre

At the end of the 1st century BC, Arles had the honour of receiving one of the first stone theatres built outside Rome. It could seat up to 10,000 spectators. The choice of Arles, and the richness of the theatre's ornamentation, testify to the importance of the city at this time. Unfortunately there has been a considerable amount of damage, as the stones were used to build the first early Christian basilica. Only two of its tall Corinthian columns could be restored to their original position. In summer, the plays of the Festival des Rencontres d'Arles are staged here.

Primatiale Saint-Trophime

You can see its belltower sticking up behind the Roman theatre. Bearing the name of the first bishop of Arles, the cathedral on Place de la République dates mainly from the 12th and 14th centuries, and is a perfect example of southern French late-Romanesque style. Its portal, sculpted in 1150, is a veritable masterpiece. The interior is more eclectic, with splendid decoration, Aubusson tapestries and two early Christian sarcophagi from the 4th and 6th centuries. The first, in the Chapelle Saint-Genest, depicts the crossing of the Red Sea. The cloister next to the church was reserved for the canons. It is one of the finest in the south of France, richly decorated with arcades of double columns and carved capitals. Around it are a chapter house, an upstairs dormitory and refectory.

Also on Place de la République, the town hall is topped by a Renaissance clock tower remaining from an earlier building. When it was inaugurated in 1676, a 3rd-century Roman obelisk excavated from the amphitheatre was erected here "to the greater glory of King Louis XIV".

Museon Arlaten

In Rue de la République, the Arles Museum is housed in the 16th-century Hôtel Laval-Castellane. It recalls Frédéric Mistral, who won the Nobel Prize for Literature in 1904 and used the prize money to finance this museum. It depicts all facets of Arlesian life in bygone times, with panels written by the poet's own hand.

Nearby are the subterranean galleries called the Cryptoportiques. Dating from 40 BC, they were the foundations of the Roman forum and are the oldest vestiges of the colony.

Palais de Luppé on Rond-Point des Arènes, was a hospice where Van Gogh stayed for a while. Now it has been converted into a Foundation dedicated to the painter and displays works by great contemporary artists.

Down to the Rhône

The famous Café Van Gogh, painted corn-yellow, is fronted by a sunny terrace on Place du Forum, a pleasant square shaded with plane trees around a statue of Frédéric Mistral.

To the north, you can see the *caldarium*, or hot room, surviving from the Baths of Constantine, built alongside the Rhône in the 4th century.

Practically opposite, the Musée Réattu has been installed in the former Renaissance priory of the Order of the Knights of Malta. Its handsome rooms are essentially devoted to 18th and 19th century works by the Provençal school, but there's a small collection of Picassos and some late 17th-century Flemish tapestries from the series the *Seven Wonders of the World*.

Musée d'Arles antique

In a big modern building on the outskirts of the town, the Museum of Ancient Arles houses one of France's finest archaeological collections. Steles, bas-reliefs, statues and sculptures, everyday objects and amphorae of every size and shape recount the Roman era in Arles, without forgetting its Celto-Ligurian origins. There is a copy of the famous *Venus of Arles* (the original, discovered in the 17th century and presented to Louis XIV to adorn his château in Versailles, is now in the Louvre), a magnificent collection of mosaics, together with Roman and early Christian marble sarcophagi—all finely carved with pagan and biblical scenes. Scale models of the main Roman buildings in the town give a good idea of their importance.

VAN GOGH

In 1888, two years after meeting the Impressionists, Van Gogh set off for Provence. He rented a small room in Arles and threw himself enthusiastically into painting. Thrilled by his discovery of perfect light, he produced canvas after canvas and dreamt of setting up an "artists' home". Suffering from solitude, he persuaded Gauguin to join him, but he left after a serious quarrel. Dismayed by the incident, Van Gogh cut off his own ear in a fit of insanity. He had himself admitted to the psychiatric clinic at Saint-Rémy, stayed there for a year and rediscovered the joy of painting: the wheatfields outside his window and the irises in the flowerbeds provided subjects for some of his best-loved pictures. In May 1890 he went back to Paris. His brother Theo found him a place to stay at Auvers-sur-Oise where, a few months later, he had another fit and committed suicide.

Fishing for shrimps on a pond in the Camargue.

Les Alyscamps

Southwest of the town centre, the Alyscamps (Elysian Fields in the Provençal dialect) was a Gallo-Roman necropolis, laid out along the Via Aurelia outside the city ramparts. A shrine was built here to the martyr Saint Genest, a Roman clerk-of-the-court who was beheaded near Arles. From the 4th century onwards, with the spread of Christianity the Alyscamps expanded to become a huge cemetery. It was one of the stages on the Pilgrims' Way to Santiago de Compostela and remained in use until the French Revolution. Both Van Gogh and Gauguin painted views of this site with its special light. Unfortunately part of the Alyscamps was damaged by construction of the railway line and workshops in the 19th century.

Abbaye de Montmajour

You can see from afar the abbey's high walls and crenellated towers. Founded in the 10th century on the site of a superb pre-Roman hermitage northeast of Arles, it grew rapidly in importance thanks to numerous donations. The rather severe church, the crypt and the cloister recalling that of Saint-Trophime in Arles date mainly from the 12th century, while the fortifications, in particular the Tour des Abbés, were built at the end of the Hundred Years' War, during the 14th century.

Saint-Gilles

This small town in the *département* of the Gard, on the western edge of the Camargue, is renowned for the magnificent Romanesque portal of its abbey church. Strongly influenced by classical architecture with Ionian and Corinthian columns, it is covered with scenes from the Old and New Testaments: Christ in Majesty at the centre, the Adoration of the Magi on the left, the Crucifixion on the right—a rare subject in Romanesque art. The tomb of Saint Gilles is in the crypt: in the Middle Ages it was considered the fourth most holy place of Christendom, on the road to Santiago de Compostela.

Camargue Regional Natural Park

Created in 1970, the park covers more or less the same area as the Grande Camargue, between the two branches of the Rhône. Your first stop should be the Information Centre at Pont-de-Gau on the road to Saintes-Maries-de-la-Mer. The neighbouring bird park stays open until sunset. Three walking trails of lengths varying from 30 to 90 minutes bring you close to the birdlife, in particular the pink flamingos. There are also aviaries sheltering injured birds that are nurtured back to health.

PINK FLAMINGOS

In 1969 there were only 500 pink flamingos in the Camargue, but the flock has been steadily increasing since the 1980s and now there can be up to 50,000 in spring and summer. The number varies from year to year, depending on weather conditions. In autumn the birds fly to Turkey and Asia Minor, North and West Africa but return to the park to breed. Building raised nests of mud, they form a single colony, which has settled on the small Fangassier islet in the southeast of the park.

Etang de Vaccarès

Cut off from the sea by a barrier of dunes, this stretch of water has been protected as a special reserve since 1927. It's quite big for a "pond", covering 13,000 ha (32,000 acres) and has its own information centre at La Capelière on the northeast shore, with an exhibition on local flora and fauna. There's a short nature trail with observation platforms.

Museums

The Musée camarguais, in a farmhouse at Pont-de-Rousty, on

the road from Arles to Saintes-Maries, describes the region from its geological beginnings to modern times. A large section is devoted to the daily life of the *manadiers* in the 19th century, and you can get close to nature on the 3-km (2-mile) *sentier écologique* (nature trail).

Further south, beside the Petit Rhône, the 19th-century Château d'Avignon organizes guided visits along its tree-lined paths. The Panorama du Voyage is a private museum dedicated to the world of gypsies and fairgrounds.

At the eastern edge of the park, south of Sambuc, the rice producers of Petit Manusclat describe their activities in the Musée du Riz de Camargue.

The shore

In the southeast, the immense Plage de Piémanson is cut off from the swamp by a ridge of dunes. Wild and windswept, it is perfect for long walks. The road leading there goes through wonderful landscapes and runs alongside the Giraud salt works. The immensity of the evaporation pools can be appreciated from a lookout point, and a miniature train travels around them.

Further west, you can reach the shore at Beauduc and further on at Pertuis-de-la-Comtesse, where there's a nudist beach at the foot of the Gacholle lighthouse. From here, walk or cycle along the 20-km (12-mile) network of paths through the marshes beside the Digue à la Mer, an earth dike built in 1859 to prevent flooding.

Saintes-Maries-de-la-Mer

Built on a lagoon at the mouth of the Petit Rhône, this town is the headquarters of the *gardian* horsemen and is renowned for its pilgrimages. Twice a year, in May and October, Roma from all over Europe come here to celebrate Saints Marie-Jacobé and Marie-Salomé, but especially Sara-la-Kâli (Sara the Black), the patron of gypsies. In summer, the little town buzzes as corridas follow upon fiestas, crowned by the Festo Vierginenco. Saintes-Maries is an excellent base for exploring the Camargue. Horseback rides are organized, as well as cruises on the Petit Rhône.

Around Town

Dedicated to the Saint Marys, the church and its sturdy bell tower dominate the town. It was built on the site of a sanctuary venerated as early as the 6th century, and was fortified in the 13th century to protect its relics from attack by Saracens and pirates. The relics are kept in the upper chapel, while the crypt contains the shrine of Sara.

In Rue Victor-Hugo, at the heart of the small and very lively traffic-free centre, the Musée Baroncelli safeguards the memory of the town and Camargue traditions.

On the sea front, a great bronze bull watches over a beach of fine grey sand, the fishing port and the marina.

Aigues-Mortes

On the edge of the Camargue, Aigue-Mortes was a significant port in the Middle Ages before the Rhône delta silted up and cut it off from the sea. It was from here that Louis IX set off on two crusades, for the first time in 1248 and again in 1270. He had ambitious plans for the newly conquered lands of Languedoc, and was keen to protect Aigues-Mortes with massive ramparts, built by his son Philippe le Hardi on the model of those at Damietta in Egypt. Soon their only purpose was to keep a considerable number of Protestants out of sight. They are remarkably well preserved and still encircle the old town centre, where tourists jostle among the souvenir shops, cafés and art galleries.

The king came to pray at the 13th-century fortified church of Notre-Dame-des-Sablons. Early Gothic in style, it was converted into a grain store and salt warehouse during the Revolution, then into a barracks during the years of the Great Terror. The Constance tower was used as a prison for a long period; you can climb it to reach the lookout posts near the parapet. The view encompasses vineyards, fields of asparagus and salt marshes—and of course the Petit Camargue which can be explored by boat or barge.

WHEN THE SAINTS CAME SAILING IN

According to legend, a boat with neither sail nor rudder ran aground here in AD 44 or 45. On board were Marie Jacobé (sister of the Virgin Mary), Marie Salomé (mother of the apostles James and John), Mary Magdalene, Lazarus, Martha and Maximin, who were fleeing to France from Palestine. They brought Christianity to Roman Gaul, first converting the gypsy people who lived here under the authority of a leader named Sara. Other versions claim that Sara was a servant of the Marys and arrived with them, or that she was an Egyptian abbess in Libya, or that she rescued the Marys from a storm at sea. She is greatly revered by the *gitans*, who, on May 24, come in their thousands to carry her statue to the sea. The following day after Mass, the *gardians* bring the saints' processional boat to the sea, a symbol of their arrival in this pagan land.

Salon-de-Provence

Extending the Camargue to the east is the Plaine de la Crau, with several industries grouped around the Etang de Berre. Salon-de-Provence, on its eastern edge, has undergone rapid development in recent times, though the centre still has a certain discreet charm. Salon was built around a rock, the Empéri, where the bishops of Arles lived in a castle from the 10th to the 17th centuries. It is the oldest feudal castle in Provence and today houses a huge museum of military art and history. Down below, the church of Saint-Michel has a fine 13th-century portal of mixed Romanesque and Gothic influence.

Nearby, Rue Nostradamus is named after its most illustrious inhabitant, with a plaque stating that "Michel Nostradamus, astrologer, doctor ordinary to the King" lived here. His house, now a museum, illustrates scenes from his life.

Rue de l'Horloge leads to a clocktower built in the 17th century over an ancient gate in the ramparts: it leads on to the intriguing Fontaine moussue, so overgrown with cushions of moss it looks like a giant mushroom. From there, Rue des Frères-Kennedy takes you to the Gothic collegiate church of Saint-Laurent (14th–15th centuries) where Nostradamus is buried.

The craggy profile of Montagne Sainte-Victoire.

Soap-makers

Outside the town centre, on avenue Donnadieu, the Musée de Salon-de-Provence et de la Crau documents the manufacture of a product much appreciated by French housewives, Marseille soap. Salon was one of the main producers. Only two factories, Fabre and Rampal, have withstood the test of time and still carry on the traditional methods of soap-making. Fabre also has a museum, the Musée du Savon de Marseille.

Côte Bleue

The port of Martigues straddles three canals and an island between the Mediterranean and the Etang de Berre. It is the departure point for a spectacular excursion along the coast to Marseille. Stretching over 24 km (15 miles) through a nature reserve, the parched and rugged Estaque chain plunges into the sea in great accordion folds, forming a series of *calanques* eaten away by erosion. They shelter a number of lively seaside resorts: first Sausset-les-Pins and Carry-le-Rouet, popular with families, each with a marina and a small beach. Then you reach La Redonne with its delightful port and Niolon with its diving school. Both of them face Marseille, in two *calanques* with weekend cottages scattered in haphazard fashion over the rocks.

Aix-en-Provence

In the midst of vineyards at the foot of Cézanne's beloved Montagne Sainte-Victoire, Aix-en-Provence is only 30 km (19 miles) from Marseille. It is a large town, with 130,000 inhabitants, but the old centre, the tree-lined boulevards, the 101 fountains and the colourful markets are for many the very essence of Provence. Its speciality is the *calisson*, a lozenge-shaped marzipan and candied melon sweet that you'll notice in many shop windows, tastefully packaged in its matching white box.

Aix is proud of its illustrious past: it was the first Roman town in Gaul in 123 BC, appreciated for its hot springs even before the conquest. It went on to become the capital of the earldom of Provence, seat of the brilliant court of le Bon Roi René (Good King René). Every July, Aix hosts a renowned music festival—*art lyrique*—mostly opera and operetta.

NOSTRADAMUS (1503–66)

The eldest son of a rich merchant, Michel de Nostredame was born in Saint-Rémy-de-Provence. At the age of 20, he went to Avignon University before going on to Montpellier, where he was awarded his doctorate of medicine in 1533. He worked on remedies for the plague, which he had tried to treat in the Languedoc in 1526. When his first Almanachs were published in 1550, he changed his name to Nostradamus and moved to Salon-de-Provence where he was to end his days. The work which would make him famous, *Les Centuries*, appeared in 1555 (*centuries* refers to the 100 verses in each of the ten chapters). Written in a style so obscure that the lines lend themselves to all manner of interpretation, the book predicted the future of the world and all the people in it, beginning with the death of Henri II's three sons without an heir to succeed them. Summoned to court by Catherine de Medici, he became the doctor of the young Charles IX, who visited him at Salon in 1564.

Cours Mirabeau

The main thoroughfare in the town centre is the Cours Mirabeau, built on the site of the old ramparts in the middle of the 17th century. It separates the old town to the north from the Mazarin district to the south. No sooner was the street laid out than the aristocracy hastened to have their mansions built along it. In classic or baroque style, they still stand behind the rows of plane trees, watching over the lively outdoor cafés. Cézanne and Blaise Cendrars used to sit at the Café des Deux Garçons at no. 53. Of the three fountains in the stretch between the Rotonde and the statue of King René, the most dramatic is the Fontaine moussue (1734) in the middle, gushing hot water from a spring at 34°C.

Old Town

From the Fontaine moussue, follow Rue Nazareth and then Rue Espariat to reach Place d'Albertas, a small paved esplanade making a fine baroque ensemble that has hardly changed since the 18th century. The Musée d'Histoire Naturelle, with a reputed collection of dinosaur eggs, is close by in the Hôtel Boyer d'Eguilles (1672).

Everyone heads for Place Richelme, where the daily market is held under the shade of plane trees, and on to the neighbouring Place de la Mairie, arguably the most attractive in Aix with its lively cafés, its large fountain topped by a Roman column and its flower market (held on Tuesdays, Thursdays and Saturdays). The Hôtel de Ville, built in the second half of the 17th century, has a decorative Italianate façade and a tower with an astronomical clock.

From the square, follow Rue Gaston de Saporta to the Musée du Vieil Aix (Museum of Old Aix) in the late-17th-century Hôtel d'Estienne de Saint-Jean at no. 17. Further along is the cathedral of Saint-Sauveur. It was founded in the early Christian era and incorporates bits of recycled Roman monuments. The baptistery dates back to the year 500, though the main part of the building is from the 11th to 15th centuries. It has numerous treasures: a superb 12th-century Romanesque cloister, a Gothic polychrome choir, Nicolas Froment's famous *Burning Bush Triptych*, tapestries and carved doors from the early 16th century (visits on request at the Sacristy).

Mazarin District

This district was named in honour of the famous Cardinal's brother, himself an archbishop. Laid out on a grid pattern, it has several *hôtels particuliers*. For an overview, walk down Rue Cabassol towards the Hôtel de Caumon, now housing the Conservatoire d'Aix. In parallel Rue du 4 Septembre, look in at the ceramics museum, Musée de Faïences Paul-Arbaud, open in the afternoons. At the bottom of this street you reach Place des Dauphins, named after its central fountain featuring four dolphins. From here, Rue Cardinal takes you to the Musée Granet at no. 17, next door to the 12th-century fortified Gothic church of Saint-Jean-de-Malte. The museum is devoted to fine arts, covering a long period from ancient Egypt up to the 19th century. There are several canvases by Paul Cézanne, including a *Montagne Sainte-Victoire*. To follow in the artist's footsteps, ask at the tourist office for documentation on the Cézanne Route.

Montagne Sainte-Victoire

Rising east of Aix and culminating at 1,011 m (3,316 ft) at the Pic des Mouches, the mountain is a long rocky ridge wrinkled by geological folds, surrounded by vineyards and *garrigue*. If everyone is familiar with the name, it is thanks to Cézanne, who painted it many times. You can find the places where he set up his easel by following a minor road winding between olive trees and poppies in the direction of Tholonet, a quiet village with a mill and castle and a splendid view of the mountain. In recent years Sainte-Victoire has been in the news because a unique deposit of dinosaur eggs was found there. The Maison de la Sainte-Victoire at Saint-Antonin-sur-Bayon has an exhibition devoted to geology and palaeontology. The climb up to the Croix de Provence, altitude 945 m (3,100 ft), is well worth the effort for the view, but it will take you at least 3 hours.

Marseille

France's second city, home to 810,000 Marseillais, is the biggest port on the Mediterranean, and the eighth in the world. Marseille has a foot in two worlds, mainland Europe and maritime Mediterranean. Founded by Greeks in the 6th century BC, it is 2,600 years old, in fact the oldest town in France. Over the centuries, it has developed a strong and pithy character, depicted notably in the works of Marcel Pagnol. Today its colourful Provençal identity is heavily spiced with the exotic influence of the large immigrant population, mostly originating in Morocco, Algeria and Tunisia but also other former French colonies in Africa. The Marseillais adore their city as much as Liverpudlians love theirs, supporting with an inordinate fervour the blue and white colours of "OM", the Olympique de Marseille.

The Old Port of Marseille, bouillabaisse and echoes of Pagnol.

Vieux Port

The Greek colonists stepped ashore at the end of a narrow gully they called Lacydon, near today's harbour at the bottom of Marseille's most famous thoroughfare, the Canebière. The avenue begins at the Quai des Belges, at the narrow end of the Old Port. Early in the morning, fishwives sell the catch of the day—sea-bass, red mullet, scorpion fish, sea urchins—everything you need to make a *bouillabaisse*. Boats leave from here for trips to the Calanques, the Riou islands and the Côte Bleue.

The south side of the harbour, all along Quai Rive Neuve, is lined with restored 18th-century warehouses, restaurants, bars and a succession of ships' chandlers. The port is bristling with masts, packed with yachts and fishing boats. A small shuttle, pompously called "le ferry boat", crosses to and fro between Place aux Huiles and the Hôtel de Ville on the north quay. But before you embark, walk on to the massive Saint-Nicolas fort, built by Louis XIV at the entrance of the Vieux Port to control the town: the view from there is breathtaking.

Le Panier

On the north side of the harbour, the Quai du Port is more modern, having been rebuilt after bombardment in World War II. The lovely baroque Hôtel de Ville escaped unscathed. Behind is the working-class district of Le Panier, clinging to the hill. Colourful buildings, washing hanging out to dry, children playing in the street: this is the timeless side of Marseille.

The 16th-century Maison Diamantée—its front wall faced with stones faceted like diamonds—houses the Musée du Vieux-Marseille, with exhibitions documenting traditions and local history. Climb the Montée des Accoules and a tangle of side-streets behind the museum to reach La Vieille Charité, a baroque hospice built in the 17th and 18th centuries to take care of the town's homeless poor. It is a superb three-storey construction, with galleries surrounding a courtyard, and nowadays houses two museums. The MAAOA is dedicated to African, Pacific and Amerindian arts, while the other, the Musée d'Archéologie Méditerranéenne, has a fine collection of artefacts from Liguria, Greece, the Middle East, Ancient Egypt, Etruria and Rome.

Cathédrale Notre-Dame de la Major

Before returning to the Vieux-Port, make a detour by way of the cathedral of La Major, below on Quai de la Joliette. Rebuilt in 1852 in neo-Byzantine style, it is immense, 141 m (463 ft) from one end to the other and 60 m (197 ft) high from the base to the cross topping the dome. When it was renovated in the 19th century, a 5th-century octagonal baptistery was discovered, the largest in France, with each side measuring 25 m (82 ft).

On your way back, you'll pass Fort Saint-Jean, guarding the Vieux-Port from the north, opposite Fort Saint-Nicolas.

La Canebière

Perpendicular to the Quai des Belges, this legendary boulevard cuts through the very heart of Marseille. Crowded with traffic and pedestrians, it is surrounded by lively streets and shopping centres. The biggest one, Centre Bourse, gives access to the Jardin des Vestiges, which used to be a sheltered anchorage behind the main port. When the car park for the Centre Bourse was excavated, workmen discovered the remains of quays and the remarkably preserved wreck of a Roman merchant ship of the 1st century. This discovery led to the creation of the fascinating Musée de l'Histoire close by, where the ship is the principal exhibit. The first centuries of the town's existence are evoked through archaeological finds and amphorae fished up from wrecks of Greek ships. The Musée de la Marine is a short walk away, in the neoclassical Bourse (Stock Exchange).

Cantini Museum

Further along La Canebière, turn right into the pedestrian shopping street of Saint-Ferréol, which leads to the Musée Cantini d'Art Moderne (19 rue Grignan). The collections give a good overview of modern painting, from Bacon, Dufy and Max Ernst to Kupka and Kandinsky, not forgetting works by local artists such as Mathieu Verdilhan, who loved the Vieux-Port.

Musée des Beaux-Arts

Northeast of the town centre, at the end of boulevard Longchamp following on from the Canebière, the Musée des Beaux-Arts occupies the left wing of the stately Palais Longchamp, built at the end of the 19th century. Its vast rooms display works by painters and sculptors of the French, Flemish, Italian and Provençal schools.

Notre-Dame-de-la-Garde

It would be unthinkable to come to Marseille without making a short visit to Notre-Dame-de-la-Garde, the "Bonne-Mère" of the Marseillais. Visible from the entire town, the basilica is perched at 154 m (505 ft) on the top of a hill to the south of the Vieux-Port. In Romano-Byzantine style, it is clad to the very tips of its cupolas with superb mosaics. The base of its walls are heaped up with thousands of ex-voto offerings, left here in thanks for answered prayers. The view from the square in front of the church is unbeatable.

Corniche and Beaches

Past the entrance to the Vieux-Port, to the south, the coast unfurls a spectacular succession of cliffs and creeks, with houses and blocks of flats clinging to them like limpets. Drive along the Corniche Président Kennedy, past the offshore Frioul islands, and you'll come to the picturesque little port of Vallon des Auffes, with fish restaurants and brightly painted fishing boats. Further on, the road comes to the Marseillais' favourite resort, the Parc balnéaire du Prado, with six artificial beaches reclaimed from the sea thanks to the excavation of the metro.

Musée d'Art Contemporain

From the beach, the Avenue du Prado slices inland to the Stade Vélodrome, the Palais des Congrès and the Musée d'Art Contemporain at 69, Avenue Haïfa. You can't miss it: outside sticks up a giant thumb by local sculptor César (who designed the French equivalent to the Oscars).

Iles du Frioul

A shuttle boat operates between the Vieux Port and the Iles du Frioul at the entrance to Marseille's harbour. In the 19th century they were used as a quarantine station and as shipyards. Every single tree was cut down, leaving the large limestone rocks bare to the harsh rays of the sun. Apart from the crystalline waters of the creeks, you can see traces of the old installations, the port on île Pomègues and the Caroline hospital on île Ratonneau. High on its lonely rock, built on the orders of François I in 1524, the Château d'If owes its fame to Alexander Dumas's novel *The Count of Monte-Cristo*. However, the island and its prison have had some illustrious inmates in their time, such as the rhinoceros immortalized by Dürer, as no one could find a more suitable home for it!

Les Calanques

Between Marseille and Cassis, the rugged limestone coastline disintegrates into a regiment of cliffs whittled away by the pounding waves. The *calanques* are deep clefts in the rocks forming narrow creeks and bays, with clear turquoise water at their foot and scented Aleppo pines rooted in their fissures. Going from west to east, the first ones are Sormiou and Morgiou—where the Cosquer cave and its 27,000-year-old wall paintings were discovered in 1991 (not open to the public). Then Sugiton and, closer to Cassis, En-Vau, Port-Pin, and Port-Miou. The easiest way to reach the *calanques* is by sea; boats leave from the Vieux Port in Marseille and from Cassis every weekday in summer and at weekends during the rest of the year (but only in fine weather). You can also hike the 28-km (17-mile) path, GR 98, from Callelongue to Cassis.

CASSIS TO HYÈRES

From Cassis to Toulon, La Sainte-Baume, Toulon, Hyères, Iles d'Hyères

The western section of the Côte d'Azur becomes gradually less jagged and the landscape softens as it leaves behind the traditional side of Provence. The resorts along this stretch of the coast are friendly and popular with families, less chic and glitzy than those further east. Off shore, the Iles d'Hyères are fragments of paradise.

From Cassis to Toulon

The Côte d'Azur starts officially at Cassis. Sandwiched between the *calanques* and the cliffs of Cap Canaille, the highest in Europe, the little port has a timeless charm. On the Quai des Baux, outdoor cafés cluster together at the foot of a ruined 13th-century castle, beside the harbour bobbing with painted boats and fishing craft. As night falls, the fishy, spicy aroma of *bouillabaisse* wafts through the air, glasses filled with fresh local wine tinkle at the Bar de la Marine, straight out of a Pagnol film. People play *boules* or sunbathe on the beach, a crescent of sand and pebbles. Boats with or without glass-bottom leave the harbour for trips to the *calanques*. You can also walk there and take a boat back, or vice-versa.

Cap Canaille

Beyond Cassis, the twisting, narrow Route des Crêtes quickly soars up the side of the cliffs, their sheer walls plunging down 416 m (1,365 ft) to the sea. The views are simply fantastic. Once past Cap de l'Aigle, the road descends to La Ciotat and its naval dockyards.

Around Bandol

Between La Ciotat and Toulon, there are several family seaside resorts, appreciated for their beaches and lively summer entertainment: Les Lecques and the nearby Aqualand at Saint-Cyr-sur-Mer; Bandol and Sanary-sur-Mer with its fishing port and palm-shaded port. Opposite Bandol, Bendor island, 10 minutes away, has plenty of tourist facilities, and a wine and spirits museum, the Musée du Vin et des Spiritueux. The île des Embiez, facing the Cap Sicié peninsula, belongs to the Ricard family (manufacturers of *pastis*), and has a museum devoted to Mediterranean oceanography.

Inland, tiny villages with narrow streets dot the landscape, covered with vineyards planted among *restanques*, terraces supported by dry stone walls.

La Sainte-Baume

Further inland, the Massif de la Sainte-Baume is like an oasis of limestone carpeted in forest. Mary Magdalene is said to have retreated to do penance in a grotto (*baoumo* in Provençal) on its slopes, and it has since become a place of pilgrimage. Her relics were mislaid in the 8th century and rediscovered in 1279 by Charles II of Anjou, Count of Provence and nephew of Louis IX. He decided to build a basilica to house the relics at the very place where they were brought to light, at Saint-Maximin. The Gothic edifice was built in stages between the 13th and 16th centuries. You can see some beautiful sculpted sarcophagi in the crypt, on the site of the old oratory, including those of the first bishop of Aix, Maximin, his successor Sidoine, the Holy Innocents (3rd century), and of course the one attributed to Mary Magdalene herself. Right next to them are two 4th-century funerary plaques with carved inscriptions, unique outside of Rome. Adjoining the basilica, the Dominican Convent is noteworthy for its superb 15th-century cloister.

Toulon

Its history revolves around its harbour. This deep coastal anchorage, protected from the winds by Mount Faron, 584 m (1,916 ft) and from the waves by the long Saint-Mandrier peninsula, it is one of the finest natural harbours of the Mediterranean. The Romans made use of it, producing the famous purple of Imperial togas here from a variety of sea snail. When the earldom of Provence was united to France, ancient Télo, later Tolo, then Tholon, became the home of the Royal Navy, driven out of the silted-up port of Aigues-Mortes. It stayed here for good. Even today, most of the battleships of the French Navy lie at anchor in the harbour. Toulon was badly bombed in 1944 and today it is a modern industrial town with a small lively core, particularly on Cours La Fayette when the morning market is in full swing.

Around Town

The heart of Toulon beats loudest around the attractive Place Puget with its plane trees, pavement cafés and the great fountain of the 18th-century Halle aux Grains (Corn Market). A network of narrow streets links it with Cours La Fayette and the market, one of the liveliest in Provence. The Musée du Vieux-Toulon at no. 69 relates the history of the town. Further south, past a great barrier of apartment blocks, you arrive at the quays and the port, stretching into the distance with its yachts and cargo vessels. On the Carré du Port, the Mairie d'Honneur was rebuilt around a door that survived the demise of the old Hôtel de Ville. It dates from the 17th century and is supported by two atlantes, *Force* and *Fatigue*, by the sculptor Puget.

Following Quai de Stalingrad to the west, you come to Place Monsenergue and the Musée de la Marine, the largest of the French Mediterranean coast.

The Harbour

In all, the harbour has been protected by 24 fortifications, some of them designed by Vauban at the height of the town's success: the Tour Royale (1514), standing at the Pointe de la Mître and housing a naval exhibition; Fort Saint-Louis (1696), further east on the way to the four artificial beaches at Mourillon; and Fort Balaguier on the other side of the harbour at La Seyne-sur-Mer, where there's another naval museum. But none of these can compete with a boat trip round the harbour, taking you close to the biggest buildings of the Arsenal.

Mont Faron

In the Middle Ages the authorities placed watchtowers all round Toulon to give advance warning in case of attack from the sea. This site could hardly be better: the summit of Mont Faron, 584 m (1,916 ft) high, affords an unbeatable view over the harbour. To reach it you can drive along the winding one-way road, a round-trip of 18 km (11 miles), or take the cable car. There are several pleasant paths and hiking trails in the garrigue, among them the "sentier des crêtes".

Hyères

By the end of the 19th century, Europe's rich and famous were flocking to Hyères: in 1892, Queen Victoria, patriotic to the end, stayed at the Hôtel Albion. But when sea-bathing became the fashion, holidaymakers looked elsewhere, for the town was haughtily perched on a hill too far from the coast. Things improved in the 1920s when a a few villas in a vaguely oriental style were built further down the slopes near the sea. But it wasn't until family tourism developed that the resort of Hyères came into its own.

Old Town

Founded in the Middle Ages, the hillside town still has some of the original 14th-century pink sandstone gates that pierced the ramparts. On Place Massillon, cafés sit at the foot of the grey-stone Tour Saint-Blaise, the only vestige of a castle occupied by the Knights Templar in the 12th and 13th centuries. It now houses an exhibition on medieval military and religious orders.

Stairs climb up to Rue Sainte-Catherine and the collegiate church of Saint-Paul, known for its collection of ex-voto offerings, the oldest piece dating from 1613. The church backs onto the Porte Saint-Paul, surmounted by a magnificent Renaissance house. Higher up, the Castel Sainte-Claire is a neo-Romanesque house built in the 19th century for the man who discovered the Venus de Milo. It is surrounded by a pleasant botanical garden descending in terraces, with a view reaching the Iles d'Hyères.

Parc Saint-Bernard

Higher still, little streets take you to this Provençal garden spilling down over terraces. The villa was designed in the 1920s by Robert Mallet-Stevens for Viscount Charles de Noailles; the style was futuristic for the times, described by the owner as "interesting to live in". Temporary exhibitions are held here. Higher up, at 190 m (623 ft), are the castle ruins.

Presqu'île de Giens

A few minutes away from Hyères town centre, the Giens peninsula is a fully fledged seaside resort. It is a rare geological formation: a large rocky island linked to the mainland by a double tombolo, low bars of sand enclosing salt pans and a lagoon where pink flamingos feed. The beaches on each side are shaded by pines and get very crowded in summer. On the west side, past Hyères-Plage, Almanarre beach stretches over 6 km (4 miles) and draws windsurfers from all over Europe. The peninsula proper is ideal for cycling beneath the pines. Around the edge are the ports of La Madrague, Le Niel and La Tour-Fondue and its little fort, departure point for trips to Porquerolles island.

Iles d'Hyères

Greeks and Romans colonized the islands of Porquerolles, Port-Cros and Levant, but later they made a great hideaway for pirates. During the Renaissance, they were known poetically as the Iles d'Or, Golden Islands. Physically they are all similar, with the same rocky heartland, the same scrubland and forests of holm oaks, abandoned forts, creeks and beaches conjuring up the image of an insular, protected part of the Côte d'Azur. The Port-Cros National Park also manages the Porquerolles National Botanic Reserve, a stretch of agricultural land.

Porquerolles

The biggest of the three islands, with an area of 12.5 sq km (4.5 sq miles) and a population of around 300, Porquerolles is a 20-minute boat trip from La Tour-Fondue.

The land is agricultural, with vineyards and orchards that you can explore on foot or by bicycle. The villagers play interminable games of *pétanque* on the Place d'Armes, and the port is jammed with yachts. The massive Fort Saint-Agathe watches over the scene; it was built in 1531 to protect the islanders from invasion, but the English took it in 1739. Napoleon undertook its restoration. Now it houses an exhibition of marine archaeology, open from May to September. From the square in front of the fort you can see beyond the umbrella pines to La Courtade beach, forming three sandy crescents.

It will take longer to reach the Conservatoire botanique national méditerranéen, also open for visits from May to September, and beyond to the Plage d'Argent and Langoustier peninsula. This is linked to Porquerolles by a narrow isthmus edged by two lovely beaches: Plage blanche (white) on the north side, Plage noire (black) to the south.

Other paths lead to the signal station on the island's highest point, at 142 m (466 ft), and to the lighthouse at Cap d'Arme, above the cliffs of the south coast.

Port-Cros

The middle island, Port-Cros is easiest reached from Le Lavandou, in 45 minutes with a stop at the île du Levant. The view as you pull into port is superb, with the little harbour protected by the two forts of L'Estissac and L'Eminence. The island is uninhabited; it was the first national park in Europe to protect both land and marine environments, founded in 1963. It is entirely dedicated to nature, and the underwater views are stunning. The park office is on the harbourside; call in for information about hikes—there are 35 km (22 miles) of paths—and the submarine trail laid out in the Baie de Palud, the only place where swimming is permitted. Onland possibilities include a nature trail, a walk to the bay of Port-Man, a climb to the Vieux-Château and its fantastic view, or to the top of Mont Vinaigre, culminating at 194 m (636 ft).

Ile du Levant

Like a long boat, its stem almost touching Port-Cros, Levant is the easternmost island of the three, stretching out its rocky backbone in the sun. Drier than the other islands, it shares its charms between nudists and soldiers. Founded in 1931, Héliopolis was one of the first nudist camps in Europe. This little "sun city" is a close-knit community with all kinds of facilities, both public and private. The most popular nudist beach is the Plage des Grottes.

LE LAVANDOU TO L'ESTEREL

Le Lavandou, Saint-Tropez, Massif des Maures, Fréjus and Saint-Raphaël, L'Esterel, Haut-Var

From Hyères to Cannes, the Côte d'Azur flaunts the best-preserved part of its coastline, a narrow area tightly squeezed between seashore and mountains. Against the forested backdrop of the great Massif des Maures and smaller Esterel, towns and resorts yawn and stretch round wide bays and gulfs, Le Lavandou and Cavalaire-sur-Mer, Saint-Tropez and Fréjus. This region is a hyphen between the family-friendly holiday resorts to the west and the glittery grandeur of the east.

Le Lavandou

This resort's success was ensured by its sandy beaches and superlative setting, with a widespread bay sheltered by the mountains of Les Maures. Turn your back on the unsightly highrises and set off from the marina to Cap Bénat, riddled with unspoilt creeks and bays. Shuttle services cross over to the Iles d'Hyères. To the east, the Corniche des Maures is a scenic route along the mountainside, linking the beaches of Cavalière, Pramousquier, Canadel-sur-Mer and Cavalaire.

The old town stands aloof from the summer clamour of Saint-Tropez.

Bormes-les-Mimosas

On the heights above Le Lavandou, the old village of Bormes, founded in the 12th century, spreads over a curve in the hillsides like tiers of theatre seats turned towards the sea. A stroll through its mimosa-drenched cobbled streets, through vaulted passageways and up stairways, takes you right up to the gates of the old castle (privately owned). On Wednesday mornings, the market adds an extra touch of colour.

Saint-Tropez

On the red chairs of Sénéquier's terrace down by the harbour, or the patios of the Byblos hotel, film stars French and foreign while away their time beneath the watchful eyes of the paparazzi. Saint-Trop' is a place for revellers, with restaurants and nightclubs galore. But you'd be well advised to look beyond the glamour and seek out its hidden charms. Long before it became the holiday address of all the showbiz stars—beginning with Brigitte Bardot who bought a house here in the 1960s—this ancient fishing village was one of the most delightful places of the Côte d'Azur. A few streets inland from the port, the old town has a more authentic appeal; few visitors make it that far. Further out on the peninsula, far away from the make-up, the sunshades and the Ferraris, vineyards spread out beneath the forests of holm oak and umbrella pines, looking out over the wide blue bay.

Around Town

A colourful fish market is held every morning on Place des Herbes, where you can sit at an outdoor café and watch the throng.

At the other end of the quay, the Musée de l'Annonciade is housed in a 16th-century chapel: its collections of Impressionist and Post-Impressionist works by Van Dongen, Signac, Bonnard, Vuillard, Matisse, with some bronzes by Maillol, are among the best-known of the Côte d'Azur.

If you follow one of the narrow streets leading from the quay, you will come to the Place des Lices, where watching the games of *pétanque* can easily become a full-time occupation.

The citadel, perched on high, was built in the 16th century to protect the town and its inhabitants. Yet twice it was besieged by the Tropéziens themselves: once in 1596 when a governor took refuge there after refusing to relinquish his command, and again in 1652 during the Fronde uprising. Things are more peaceful these days and the fort is occupied by an appealing naval museum, Musée de la Marine. Naturally, there's a great view over the rooftops to the sea.

Beaches

Bouillabaisse to the west and Graniers to the east are the nearest beaches but not the best. To find the golden sands of the tourist brochures, you'll have to drive or take the shuttle bus *(navette)* from Place des Lices (there are only 4 a day). Several roads wind through the vineyards to the beaches; all of them, except

SAINT TORPES

Saint-Tropez takes its name from a Roman knight, Torpes, one of Nero's attendants. After he was converted to Christianity, the emperor had him beheaded. His body was placed between a cockerel and a dog in a boat that was left to float from Pisa at the whim of wind and waves, landing eventually one May 17 at Heraclea—the future Saint-Tropez. The Tropéziens commemorate their patron saint with a 3-day festival called *La Bravade* (May 16–18) with parades in military and naval costume, music, dancing and gun salvos.

for Canébier, are on the east side of the peninsula. A single crescent of sand stretching for 5 km (3 miles) is shared between the exotically named Tahiti, where the yachts tie up, Moorea, Bora Bora and Pampelonne.

A pleasant inland excursion through vineyards and cork oak forest takes you to the pretty village of Ramatuelle.

Port-Grimaud

In the 1960s, the marshlands deep within the Gulf of Saint-Tropez, below the medieval village of Grimaud, were filled in and developed by a French architect, François Spoerry. He created Provence's "Little Venice", a village of brightly coloured houses laced with canals. Each house has its own mooring so people can park their yacht right outside their front door.

Sainte-Maxime

Opposite Saint-Tropez on the north side of the Gulf, Sainte-Maxime is more of a family seaside resort, with its quays and a beach. Within the walls of the Tour Carrée (1520) is a Musée des Traditions Locales. In summer, a daily craft market is held in the traffic-free centre.

Beyond Sainte-Maxime, the coast is lined with attractive sandy beaches right up to the outskirts of Fréjus.

Massif des Maures

The largest massif of the Côte d'Azur, the Maures stretches for some 60 km (37 miles) between Hyères and Fréjus. Covered by forests of chestnuts, cork and holm oaks, and threaded by pathways, it culminates at the Pic de la Sauvette at 779 m (2,556 ft).

Villages in the Maures are few and far between, the principal one being La Garde-Freinet, an old Saracen bastion. Below it is Grimaud, spreading down the southern slope of the massif beneath the ghostly ruins of its feudal castle (11th–14th centuries). In the lower part of the village, see the lovely 11th-century Romanesque church of Saint-Michel, and facing it the house of the Knights Templar.

To the west, at the end of a road in a lonely valley, the charterhouse of La Verne has been home to a community of the Order of Bethlehem since 1982. The monastery was founded in 1170 but abandoned after the Revolution. Striking use has been made of serpentine, a green stone, for door and window frames and decorative features.

Fréjus and Saint-Raphaël

In the hollow between the Maures and Esterel, at the mouth of the Argens River, these twin towns embracing the lovely Bay of Fréjus have been cultivating

Where the Esterel meets the sea, the rock is dark red.

their seaside potential since Roman days. Their heyday came at the end of the 19th century, as you can guess from some of the beautiful houses, but now they have become popular resorts.

Fréjus Town Centre

The name Fréjus is derived from the ancient Forum Julii, founded by Julius Caesar in 49 BC after his conquest of Gaul. It became a bishopric with the expansion of Christianity and many religious monuments were built. They form a remarkable group in the town centre around Saint-Léonce cathedral. In early Gothic style, the cathedral dates from the beginning of the 13th century and contains a notable early-Christian octagonal baptistery of the 5th century. You can only see it as part of a guided tour, like the superb Renaissance doors of the main portal. The 13th-century cloister with magnificent columns of Carrara marble still has its original wood frames; about a third of the 1200 panels of the coffered ceiling are painted with mythical beasts and subjects of religious and ordinary daily life.

Behind the cathedral, the Musée Archéologique displays fragments of frescoes brought to light in 1988, a very fine 2nd-century mosaic depicting a leopard, and a wonderful marble bust of the Greek god Hermes with two different faces, back to back, from AD 40–50.

L'Esterel

From Saint-Raphaël to Cannes, the red porphyry of the Esterel massif tumbles into the sea in a jagged chaos of rocks and cliffs.

The coast road meanders beside the waves, clinging to the contours of the "Corniche d'Or" between piles of rocks and hidden inlets, with plenty of viewing platforms so you can stop and gasp at the panorama. In some places steps lead down to the sea. Saint-Raphaël's tourist office organizes guided hikes in conjunction with the forestry commission (Office national des Forêts).

Corniche d'Or

After a 40-minute walk, you'll get a splendid view over the coast and the tiny Ile d'Or from the signal station (Sémaphore) on the Cap du Dramont. Further round the coast is the harbour of Agay and its resort beneath by the Rastel rock, hemmed by a long sandy beach. Then the smaller Anthéor; at sunset, the view from its eastern end, over the red rocks of the Esterel, is stunning.

From the Pointe de Cap Roux, a road goes up to the Notre-Dame pass, branching out into forest trails and hiking paths to the Pic de l'Ours, the Pic du Cap Roux at 452 m (1,483 ft) and higher still to the summit of Mont Vinaigre at 618 m (2027 ft).

The last panorama along the coast is from the Pointe de l'Esquillon; a 5-minute walk from the car park takes you to a 360° view of the fiery Esterel rocks, the Gulf of Napoule and Bay of Cannes, the Iles de Lérins on the horizon.

Haut-Var

In the northern part of the Var *département*, the inland villages perch high among the forests, vineyards and olives planted on terraced platforms. With their shady streets, ancient fountains, washhouses and ruined castles, they tell the tale of a hinterland where life has changed more slowly than elsewhere. Entrecasteaux, Cotignac, Aups, Tourtour, Bargème and Mons are just a few of these delightful places lost in time.

Abbaye du Thoronet

In the lush green Argens valley, Thoronet abbey stands in the middle of a lovely forest. Founded in the 12th century, it has a superb, very restrained Romanesque church, monastic buildings and an unusual cloister with one end wider than the other. It is the most beautiful of the three great Cistercian abbeys of Provence.

CARLTON

CANNES TO MENTON

Cannes, Artists' Villages, Antibes-Juan-les-Pins, Grasse and surroundings, Nice, The Corniches, Menton, Monaco

Palaces, palmiers, promenades: this is the French Riviera. "Discovered" by the British, it is now completely cosmopolitan, and also a place that many choose to spend their retirement. Paradoxically, it is not very spacious: the towns tower up the hillsides using every precious plot of land. And the few sandy beaches are mostly artificial.

Cannes

At the beginning of the 19th century, Cannes was just a little fishing village at the foot of the Colline du Suquet dominating the Gulf of Napoule. Then the British came, mostly aristocrats in search of sun and quiet during the long winter months—the first one is said to be Lord Brougham. Luxury hotels sprang up like mushrooms, and the boulevard de La Croisette was laid out. In 1947, the first International Film Festival was held, bringing its cortège of actors, directors, writers, stars and starlets. This is the most international of French resorts and almost looks like a film set, the palm trees pefectly placed, the wedding-cake façades, the neat market stalls and the Suquet hill forming a colourful backdrop to the scene.

Stepping out in style on La Croisette.

La Croisette

The famous boulevard along the seafront unfurls a prestigious roll-call of sumptuous hotels that the French call *palaces*: the Majestic, the Noga Hilton, the Carlton, the Martinez. Nothing but chandeliered and red-carpeted luxury. Rollerbladers scoot by showing off their matching accessories, big gleaming limos glide past, women cultivate their *chic*, down to the bows on their chihuahuas. Regiments of loungers and parasols are deployed from one end of the beach to the other. But the big star is the Palais des Festivals, a modern building beside the marina where fabulous yachts lie at anchor and boats leave for the Iles de Lérins. The MIDEM (International Music Market) is held here in January, and the famous film festival in May. Filmstars have left their handprints in the pavement of the Allée des Etoiles. No doubt you'll enjoy window-shopping in Rue d'Antibes parallel to La Croisette, full of smart boutiques and antique shops.

Old Cannes

Bustling Rue Meynadier, full of shops and boutiques, is the heart of town, between the flower market in the Allée de la Liberté (opposite the port) and the Forville covered market and its stalls of fruit and vegetables, flowers, meat and fish. Small streets climb the Colline du Suquet, topped by the 12th-century castle of La Castre, once owned by the abbots of Lérins. It is now a museum, with fine ethnological and historical collections donated by travellers and explorers. The sections on Mediterranean antiquities and musical instruments are especially interesting. Go to the top of the tower for a view over the bay.

Iles de Lérins

Forming a curve at one end of the Gulf of Napoule, the islands of Sainte-Marguerite and Saint-Honorat can be reached in 20–30 minutes. At one time the only occupants were religious communities.

A hermit, Honorat, founded a monastery on the smallest island in the year 410. It was frequently attacked by pirates but somehow managed to become one of the most important in Christendom. It is still occupied by a community of Cistercian monks who cultivate vines, oranges and lavender, and produce a herbal liqueur called Lérina. You can visit the church of the present monastery and its small museum, as well as the old fortified monastery (11th–15th centuries) on a headland of the south coast. The monks took refuge in its keep whenever pirates assailed the island.

Sainte-Marguerite is a haven of peace today, but its Fort Royal once served as a prison. In fact it was here that the famous Man in the Iron Mask was locked up. No one knows his identity, some think he was the illegitimate son of Louis XIV, others say he was his brother. You can look around the cells and visit the Musée de la Mer, which displays various objects such as amphoras and glassware found off shore in the wrecks of Roman ships.

Artists' Villages

Three quiet villages above Cannes are particular favourites of artists and craftsmen: Picasso had homes in both Mougins and Vallauris, and Biot is known for its glassmakers.

Mougins

No one can resist the charm of this old village where Churchill painted watercolours and Picasso spent the last years of his life.

The last vestige of the ramparts, the Porte Sarasine, has been converted into the Musée de la Photographie, which displays a collection of ancient cameras and photographs of Picasso and the village taken by the some of the world's great photographers. Ask at the museum for the keys to the bell tower of Saint-Jacques church, next door.

The 12th-century chapel of Notre-Dame-de-Vie lies in a pastoral setting just a short way out of the village.

Vallauris

Its honorary citizen Picasso lived in Vallauris from 1948 to 1955, and with other artists he helped revive the ancient traditions of pottery-making. Half a century later, the village is overwhelmed with workshops and boutiques; a pottery festival is held in summer. Whichever way you turn you'll come across works by Picasso: the market place, officially Place Paul-Isnard, is generally known as the *Place de l'Homme au Mouton* because of its sculpture of a man with a sheep; opposite, in the castle chapel is a large fresco, *Guerre et Paix* (War and Peace) and some ceramics.

Biot

High on its hill above Antibes, this old village was also known for its pottery; in the 18th century, there were around 40 factories producing huge wine jars. Today, glass-making has taken over as the main industry, The oldest and most renowned workshop is the Verrerie de Biot, where you can watch the men making their bubbly glassware every day except Sundays.

Walking around the cobbled streets you will see remains of the ramparts and a 15th-century church on Place aux Arcades containing two altarpieces by the Niçois painter Louis Bréa (1453–1516). You can also visit the diminutive Musée d'Histoire et de Céramiques biotoises (local history and ceramics).

Southeast of the village, in the Antibes direction, the splendid Musée Fernand Léger has a spectacular façade covered by an immense multi-coloured ceramic panel. The collections cover every facet of this gifted artist's work: cubist, socialist, modernist, ceramicist, and there's a superb bas-relief of *Femmes aux Perroquets* (Women with Parrots).

Antibes–Juan-les-Pins

Cap d'Antibes is a promontory reaching into the Mediterranean like a great crooked finger. On the west side, Juan-les-Pins is known for its jazz festival. The resort curves round a long beach and has facilities for all kinds of water sports. To the north, on the road to Nice, Marineland is a water park with fantastic dolphin and killer whale shows.

Further east, Antibes is the Greek Antipolis. Its old streets cluster around the Fort Carré.

Sea Front

On Avenue Amiral-de-Grasse, you'll see the remains of the ramparts built by Vauban in the 17th century. They follow the sea front as far as the Saint-André bastion, now the site of the Musée d'Archéologie. This describes the history of the city, beginning with its foundation in the 6th century BC by the Greeks of Massalia. Exhibits include objects from daily life, amphoras and what is known as the *galet de Terpon*, a stone engraved with an inscription in ancient Greek.

There's a pleasant promenade alongside the ramparts leading north past Gravette beach to the Vieux-Port and the Port Vauban. Opposite, the Fort Carré, shaped like a four-pointed star, crowns a hill; it was built in the 16th century on the boundary of ancient Provence (guided tours only).

Picasso Museum

The Château Grimaldi is built on a small mound set back from the ramparts, first the site of the Greek acropolis and later the Roman castrum. In the summer of 1946, Picasso set up his easel here and worked non-stop for six months. When he left, he donated 300 canvases, drawings, engravings and ceramics to the town; they are exhibited here alongside works by other artists such as Miró, Arman and César.

Old Town

Near the museum, the Cathedral of the Immaculate Conception is largely baroque in style, despite some 12th-century Romanesque details. Apart from the handsome carved wooden doors, you can see Louis Bréa's altarpiece of Notre-Dame-du-Rosaire. A traditional Provençal market is held every day in summer on neighbouring Place Masséna.

Cap d'Antibes

Following the coast southwards you reach the long Plage de la Salis, ideal for swimming. Then you enter Cap d'Antibes, an area of sumptuous residences curtained by pines. For a fine panorama, go to the Garoupe lighthouse next to the chapel of Notre-Dame-du-Bon-Port (which has some lovely modern stained-glass windows). Starting at the beach of La Garoupe, the Sentier de Tirepoil is a pleasant pathway along the coast, with views over the Baie des Anges.

Two gardens are open to the public: that of the Villa Eilenroc (Tuesdays and Wednesdays), and the Jardin Thuret, 5 ha (12 acres) of Mediterranean plants.

Grasse and Surroundings

To the French, Grasse is synonymous with flowers and perfume. Its mild climate is ideal for growing jasmine, roses and thousands more essences cultivated in the area. The city supplies two-thirds of French production.

The old centre of high buildings and narrow, sloping streets and passages can be darkly sinister or irresistibly charming, when the sun lights up the terracotta walls. It makes a perfect stopover before you head for the hinterland with its rugged landscape.

Old Town

The busiest parts of Grasse are around the long Place aux Aires and the Place aux Herbes. Lined by 18th-century façades, bistros and arcades where tanners once spread out the skins, Place aux Aires is the site of the daily market. Call in at the magnificent 13th-century Romanesque cathedral of Notre-Dame-du-Puy, near the town hall, to see the altarpiece by Louis Bréa, a Fragonard and three works by Rubens.

A short way out of the centre, below the esplanade, the Villa-Musée Fragonard occupies a large town house where the artist resided during the Revolution. You can see original works by Fragonard and canvases by other members of his family. The garden is small but tranquil.

Sun, moon and stars in the village of Gourdon.

Perfume

Grasse was originally a town of leather-workers but gradually turned towards perfumery. Roses, hyacinths and jasmine were grown up to the gates of the town. Today Grasse has 30 perfumeries but only four are open to the public: Fragonard, Galimard, Molinard and the Salon des Parfums. Some offer the chance to blend your own perfume (by appointment only).

In the excellent Musée de la Parfumerie on Place du Cours you'll learn everything you ever wanted to know about distillation. You can see a model of the perfumier's *orgue*, or "organ" where all the different essences are set out in tiers of glass tubes, and an exquisite collection of bottles, vases and jars used to hold perfume since the days of Cleopatra.

On the other side of the street, the Musée Fragonard offers a similar visit with more specialized, well-displayed collections, though it is more commercial.

Nearby are two more museums, the Musée d'Art et d'Histoire de Provence, of local interest, and the enchanting Musée Provençal du Costume et du Bijou (costumes and jewellery).

Gorges du Loup

Above Grasse, the River Loup has carved out these spectacular gorges between the Plateau de Caussols and the Puy de Tourettes. You can drive along either side, along twisting roads that closely follow their contours. The village of Bar-sur-Loup at the entrance to the gorge is known for its Church of Saint-Jacques, or more precisely for its altarpiece consisting of two canvases by Louis Bréa and its late 15th-century wood painting, *Danse Macabre*.

High above the gorges, at 758 m (2,487 ft), the picturesque village of Gourdon clings like an eyrie to a high crag, huddled round a 9th-century castle with terraced gardens designed by Le Nôtre. It is consistently voted one of France's most beautiful villages and overrun with tourists.

Vence

Further east, Vence behind its high medieval walls is an outpost of Nice. The old town centre is cobbled and traffic-free, its streets lined with delightful little shops full of local products.

Built onto the ramparts, facing a great ash tree said to be 400 years old, is the château of the Barons de Villeneuve. It stages remarkable exhibitions of 20th-century art, by painters such as Matisse, Dufy, Chagall and Dubuffet, run by the Fondation Emile-Hugues.

On the road to Saint-Jeannet, the small white Chapelle du Rosaire was entirely decorated by Matisse between 1947 and 1951, at the request of Soeur Jacques-Marie, a Dominican nun who had been his model in her youth. The artist designed everything, from the candlesticks to the black line drawings on the walls and the stained-glass windows. The chapel is open for visits every afternoon (and Tuesday and Thursday mornings 10–11.30 a.m.); Sunday mass at 10 a.m. is followed by a guided tour.

The Château Notre-Dame-des-Fleurs, just west of Vence, is a delightful private gallery with collections of modern and contemporary art and a marvellous terraced sculpture garden.

Saint-Paul-de-Vence

This medieval hilltop village became a frontier town in 1388 when Nice became subject to the House of Savoy. Its charm and wonderful light made it a magnet for artists and writers during the 1920s, all of whom brought fame to its modest *auberge*, La Colombe d'Or, which has become one of France's most prestigious restaurants. Nearby is the square where actors such as Yves Montand and Lino Ventura used to play *pétanque* with the locals.

Perfectly preserved within its ramparts, the village is totally delicious, its beautiful 16th- and 17th-century grey stone houses lovingly restored to hold boutiques, workshops, restaurants and a surfeit of galleries.

If you keep heading upwards, you'll pass by the Grande Fontaine (1850), and at the top of the hill, the 12th–17th century Gothic collegiate church adorned with many works of baroque art, including a painting of Saint Catherine of Alexandria attributed to Tintoretto. Right next to it is the small Musée d'Histoire, featuring famous visitors to Saint-Paul. Chagall is buried in the cemetery at the back of the village. Gravitate down to the ramparts at sunset to see the surrounding hills blush pink.

A short walk above the village, the Fondation Maeght has a superb collection of modern art. It organizes exhibitions in rotation, with works by Miró, Braque, Giacometti and others.

La Colle-sur-Loup

For a more "authentic" village, drive or walk another 3 km (2 miles) and wander round the meandering streets of La Colle, on the hill facing Saint-Paul. On Avenue du Maréchal-Foch, the little church of Saint-Jacques has a 17th-century clocktower and an altar made from an old stone road-roller. Further down the street, call in at the gallery of La Maison des Arts, where local, mostly English-speaking artists

Saying it with flowers in Saint-Paul-de-Vence.

display paintings, sculpture and ceramics. Week-long art courses are held here, in English, in the lovely 18th-century house (for details see www.maisondesarts.com). Nestling at the foot of a forested hill, an old grey-stone abbey that once belonged to the monks of the Iles de Lérins has been converted into a fine hotel and restaurant. On September 15 La Colle organizes a Fête des Vieux Métiers, when the villagers dress in traditional costumes and demonstrate bygone trades.

Cagnes-sur-Mer

About halfway along the Baie des Anges, Cagnes has a dual personality: down by the sea is the resort of Cros-de-Cagnes, and on the hilltop is the charming *village perché* of Hauts-de-Cagnes. Its colourful streets and vaulted passageways were built around the 14th-century fort of the Grimaldis, converted into a palace in 1620. Its central courtyard is surrounded by galleries with typical Renaissance painted ceilings. The rooms house an interesting Musée de l'Olivier documenting cultivation of the olive, as well as exhibitions of modern art.

On Chemin des Collettes, facing old Cagnes and in the middle of a huge garden of gnarled olive trees, the house where Renoir spent his last years (1907–19) has been converted into a museum. You can see a reconstruction of his studio, a few paintings and old photographs, some personal objects and works by artist friends.

Nice

This most Italian of French cities is not just nice, it is bewitching. Watching over the Baie des Anges, it is held in the embrace of hills that shelter it from the mistral winds. In the 5th century BC, the Greeks of Massalia founded a trading post here called Nikaïa, then an acropolis on the rock that now looks down on the Promenade des Anglais. In the 1st century BC, the Romans built their own settlement on the Colline de Cimiez (Cemenelum). The town passed under the control of the House of Savoy in 1388 and did not become part of France until 1860. By then it was already appreciated for its mild climate, even in the middle of winter. Today, with 350,000 inhabitants, it is the fifth-largest city in France and has many sides to its character: popular, friendly, trendy, cultural, artistic, with an over-riding nostalgia for the Belle Epoque.

Promenade des Anglais

At the beginning of the 19th century, a number of English people who generally spent their winters in Nice got together to finance the construction of a path along the Baie des Anges. It was named after them, the Promenade des Anglais, and soon a host of luxury hotels sprang up along its length: the Royal, the Westminster, the West End. The Negresco, the most famous of all and now a national historic monument, was named after its Romanian founder. Down below, the beach stretches 5 km (3 miles) round the bay. It is divided into sections: from Castel, Opéra, Beau Rivage, Galion, Lido to Florida, Bambou and Miami, up to the airport. But whatever the name, every beach is the same, pebbles all the way.

One of the most interesting buildings on the Promenade des Anglais is the Palais de la Méditerranée, a former casino that went bust. All that's left of it is the white Art Deco façade (now a protected monument); behind it is a car park. The nearby Musée Masséna recounts the history of Nice in its splendid Empire rooms, with fine collection of paintings, porcelain and ceramics, and weaponry.

Vieille Ville

Beyond the Palais de la Méditerranée, the Promenade des Anglais becomes the Quai des Etats-Unis curving round as far as the castle hill. This forms the southern limit of the old town, roughly triangular in shape. Cut through one of the several passageways to the lively Cours Saleya, the market place. Fruit and vegetables are sold in the mornings, flowers in the afternoons; you can wander around munching on crispy pieces of *socca*, a chick-pea flour pancake cooked right there on the spot. The square is lined with cafés, restaurants and souvenir shops. Behind it, narrow streets lead eventually to the neoclassical Palais de Justice and the baroque cathedral of Sainte-Réparate, consecrated in 1699. It takes up one whole side of pretty Place Rossetti. This was once a craftsmen's stronghold but their workshops have been converted into boutiques and shops selling local specialities. Look out for delicious *navettes*, shuttle-shaped biscuits delicately flavoured with orange-flower water.

In Rue Droite, the 17th-century Palais Lascaris makes a handsome setting for the Musée des Arts Décoratifs baroque and its collections of ceramics, furniture and a complete 18th-century apothecary's shop. Do not miss the superb staircase with painted walls and ceiling.

Continuing along Rue Droite, you come to Place Saint-François and its daily fish market. From there, take Rue Saint-Augustin to its baroque church built in 1670. Inside is a *Piéta* by Louis Bréa.

Colline du Château

At the north end of the old town, you can climb up to the top of the castle hill by the winding stairs of the Montée Eberlé. The hill was first settled by the Celto-Ligurians, then by the colony of Greeks from Massalia. In the 12th century the Counts of Provence chose it as the site of their castle. In the 14th century, the lower town of Nice burst out of its corset of walls and began to spread up the west side of the hill, where the Old Town is today. Hardly anything remains of the early settlers; the castle was demolished in 1706 on the orders of Louis XIV. But there's a fine view over the town, over the whole length of the Promenade des Anglais to the west and the two harbours to the east, surrounded by late-19th-century houses. The only surviving fortification, the circular Tour Bellanda, contains the Musée de la Marine.

You can get back down to the seafront by the stairs or save your legs by taking the lift.

Promenade des Arts

Boulevard Jean-Jaurès forms the northern boundary of the Old Town. At its end is the Promenade des Arts, an area of state-of-the-art architecture comprising the Musée d'Art moderne et contemporain. The building is octagonal, hollow inside, with roof walks providing a 360° view of the city. The collections include works by all the great names of American and French modern art.

You can't miss the completely whacky Bibliothèque Louis-Nucéra on Place Yves-Klein. A large glass cube perched on an enormous chin and neck, it houses the public library.

Cimiez

In 14 BC, Augustus founded Cemenelum on Cimiez hill above the town. It was capital of the Roman province of Alpes Maritimae until the 4th century. Cimiez is now a residential area of beautiful Belle Epoque houses, with a huge park containing museums and antique remains. In the 19th century, the owner of the site, Comte Garin de Coconato, began excavations and unearthed a theatre, amphitheature and baths, all from the 3rd century, together with the foundations of houses and a number of early Christian artefacts (5th century). When the Count died, his wife had the dig covered over to make a kitchen garden. Many objects are displayed here in the Musée archéologique, tracing the Greek and Roman history of the area.

The Musée Matisse is housed in the lovely 17th-century terracotta-coloured Villa des Arènes, set in a large park planted with olive trees. Suffering from bronchitis, the artist came to Nice in 1917 and never left. The museum displays canvases, sculpture, tapestries and models of the Chapelle du Rosaire at Vence.

If you walk through the park behind the museum you reach the working Franciscan monastery of Cimiez. It includes a museum and the church of Notre-Dame-de-Cimiez containing several masterpieces, among them three magnificent altarpieces by Louis Bréa.

At the bottom of Cimiez hill, on Avenue Dr-Ménard, the Musée Marc Chagall exhibits a noteworthy collection of the artist's works, not only sculpture, stained glass, mosaics, tapestries and engravings but also his huge *Message Biblique* related in no less than 17 paintings.

CARNIVAL

The famous Nice Carnival was first codified in 1873, but the tradition goes back to the distant past. In the Middle Ages, it was celebrated in the period between Ephiphany and Ash Wednesday, the beginning of Lent. The costumes and floats in papier-mâché are designed on a different theme each year, generally based on current events. The king of the festivities, Sa Majesté Carnaval, is sacrified on a bonfire as the celebrations come to a close.

Musée des Beaux-Arts

In the west part of the city, the Jules-Chéret Museum of Fine Arts, at 33 avenue des Baumettes, is set in a handsome Italianate villa of 1878 built for a Ukrainian princess and bought by the town in 1925. Its first collection was donated by Napoleon III after the union of the earldom of Nice with France in 1860. It now displays Flemish paintings, sculptures by Carpeaux and Rodin, Impressionist paintings and two fine collections of Fauvist works by Van Dongen and Raoul Dufy.

Terra Amata

Near the port, the Musée de Paléontologie Humaine at 25, boulevard Carnot was built on the site of a prehistoric settlement dating back 400,000 years. Its inhabitants, apparently, used to hunt elephants.

The Corniches

Between Nice and the Italian border, the last foothills of the Alps plunge dramatically into the blue Mediterranean. Towns and villages make use of every available scrap of space. Three levels of roads run along the hillside, offering some of the most grandiose views of the Riviera. Winding between the peaks, the dizzying Grande Corniche follows the Via Aurelia of antiquity. At the middle level is the Moyenne Corniche, while the rocky, rugged seafront is warily negociated by the Basse Corniche. In places, you can pass from one level to another up or down narrow roads.

Villefranche-sur-Mer

Sheltered by the Cap Ferrat peninsula, Villefranche was first appreciated for its anchorage; the 18th-century houses in all shades of ochre, pink and yellow have done the rest. It was a favourite haunt of filmmakers from Alfred Hitchcock to Georges Lautner, but has kept its simple way of life. Near the port, the 14th-century chapel of Saint-Pierre was decorated by Cocteau “for his fishermen friends”. He painted the superb group of frescoes in 1956 and 1957. Parallel to the seafront, the mysterious Rue Obscure, with ogival and Romanesque vaulting, dates back to the town’s foundation in the 13th century. Higher up, stairs climb to the baroque church of Saint-Michel and Place de la Paix, site of a colourful market.

Above the port, the Citadelle Saint-Elme, built by a Duke of Savoy from 1557, houses the town hall and all the museums. These are the Fondation-Musée Volti, dedicated to the sculptor

The modern district of Nice climbs the hill above the port.

Antoniucci Volti (1915–89), known for his voluptuous bronze nudes; the Musée d'Art et d'Histoire, the Collection Goetz-Boumeester (paintings and engravings), the Collection Roux with historic figurines and the wreck of a 16th-century ship.

Cap Ferrat

The long peninsula covered in pine trees separates Villefranche harbour from the Baie des Fourmies. This paradise for millionaires has two beaches, Passable and Paloma, a picturesque port at Saint-Jean-Cap-Ferrat, and several exotic gardens. Two of them are open to the public, that of the Villa des Cèdres, once owned by Leopold II, king of the Belgians, and that of the Villa Ile-de-France, built in 1912 in Italian Renaissance style. It belonged to the Baroness Ephrussi (née Rothschild), whose collection of Sèvres porcelain is displayed in the villa. The gardens, covering 4 ha (10 acres), are divided into seven sections, the main one being a French formal garden with ponds and fountains, shaped like the bridge of a boat. The other gardens are in various styles ranging from Provençal, Florentine and Andalusian to Japanese.

Beaulieu-sur-Mer

At the foot of high cliffs, Beaulieu is a rather chic resort on the Baie des Fourmies. You can visit the elegant Villa Kérylos, built by the politician Théodore Reinach from 1902 to 1908. He was passionately interested in archaeology and designed his house on the style of an ancient Greek palace, much as he must have imagined the palace of King Minos at Knossos. The columns, mosaics, frescoes, down to the furnishings, draperies and bathroom fittings, everything is simply exquisite.

Eze

You can drive to Eze along the Moyenne Corniche, but you have to climb the last lag, up the winding narrow path to this old stone village crouching on the summit of a rocky outcrop. A labyrinth of lanes and vaulted passageways lead left and right past the ancient houses, many of which have been converted into boutiques and craft shops. At the top is a church, and an exotic cactus garden where more than 400 succulents flourish. The view sweeps over the rooftops to the sea, 400 m (1,312 ft) down below.

From the bottom of the village, the Sentier Friedrich-Nietzsche descends in tight hairpin bends to Eze-sur-Mer, a walk of 30 to 45 minutes. This is where the philosopher found the inspiration for the third part of his work *Thus spake Zarathustra*.

La Turbie

At the highest point of the Via Julia Augusta above the Principality of Monaco, the village of La Turbie used to mark the frontier between Roman Italy and colonized Gaul. In 5 BC, a monument called the *Trophée des Alpes* was erected to commemorate the conquest of the Alps by Emperor Augustus. Originally it stood 50 m (164 ft) high and looked like a gigantic white-iced wedding cake with a square base and a round, domed top tier surrounded by a colonnade. Today only a section of the western wall survives, with four columns and part of the base. A small museum explains the monument's history.

Roquebrune

On the cliffside between Basse and Moyenne corniches, the village clusters round a rocky peak topped by a 10th-century castle. Make your way to the delightful little Place des Deux-Frères for a truly breathtaking view of the coast. As you wander around the maze of narrow streets, lined with artists' workshops, you'll discover the church of Sainte-Marguerite; the vaulted passages of Rue de la Fontaine end up at a venerable olive tree said to be 1,000 years old—an extraordinary tangle of trunks and roots.

The footpath narrows into a track and goes down to Cap Martin, covered with smart houses. Promenade Le Corbusier traces the west side of the peninsula all the way to Saint-Romain.

Vallées des Paillons

The villages of the Paillons Valleys were built at the top of impregnable peaks, to keep them safe from Saracen raids. The most beautiful is perhaps Peillon, its grey stone houses hunched up on a rocky outcrop skirted by green meadows. Peille climbs in terraces up to the foot of its ruined castle, while Lucéram's church of Sainte-Marguerite is worth a visit to see its fine altarpieces. Coaraze is known as the sunniest village in France; on the façade of the town hall is a sun dial designed by Jean Cocteau. Further east, wrapped around a rock crowned with the ruins of a medieval castle, Sainte-Agnès watches over Menton from a dizzying 650 m (2,132 ft).

Menton

If you think Menton has something of an Italian atmosphere, that's only natural, as it belonged to Italy until 1861. Its ochre houses rise in tiers between the mountains and the sea front. Called the "garden city", it enjoys 316 days of sun each year, and like the rest of the Côte d'Azur, it has been a favourite with artists for at least two centuries.

Sea Front

Around the Baie du Soleil, the promenade lines a pebble beach. People stroll up and down, past the casino and Belle Epoque hotels now converted into private residences. On the Esplanade du Bastion, a 17th-century fort has been converted into the Musée Jean-Cocteau. Novelist, playwright, film director, artist, illustrator, Cocteau (1889–1963) preferred to call himself a poet. He supervised the restoration of the building and designed the interior, from the showcases down to the pebble mosaics at the entrance (using pebbles from the local beach). The displays include drawings, ceramics, a large tapestry of Judith coming out of Holofernes' tent, and his last work, the series of coloured drawings called the *Innamorati*, the Lovers of Menton.

From here, follow Quai Napoléon II, which closes one side of the Vieux-Port. The panorama is splendid, revealing the gentle stretches of sand of the Plage des Sablettes on the Baie de Garavan.

Old Town

Set back from the sea front, the covered market (1896) is open daily; the stalls spilling into the surrounding streets on Saturdays. Just behind here, traffic-free Rue Longue is the backbone of old Menton, lined with street cafés and boutiques, dotted here and there with little squares.

Higher up, the graceful 17th-century baroque church of Saint-Michel looks over the roofs of the old town and the Baie de Garavan. On the same esplanade is the 17th-century chapel of the Pénitents-Blancs (White Penitents).

Further west is the Musée de la Préhistoire Régional and the town hall, known for its Salle des Mariages (wedding room) entirely decorated by Cocteau in 1958.

Parks and Gardens

In February, the floats of the Lemon Festival are paraded in the Jardins Biovès behind the casino, but this is more of a promenade than a fully fledged park. You will probably prefer the flowery tranquillity of Jardin Val-Rahmeh, set out on terraces around a villa above the Baie de Garavan. The neighbouring Jardin des Colombières is typically Mediterranean, with cypresses and olives.

At the other end of Menton on the road to Gorbio, the Serre de la Madone is a magnificent botanical collection begun by an English major, with a great many species from Asia.

Monaco

Monaco rhymes with glitz and glamour, glossy magazines, luxury yachts and Formula 1. Though there's no customs post at the frontier, it is a state in its own right (under the protection of France), with its own coat of arms, its own red and white flag, its language and traditions. Only 7,000 of the 32,000 inhabitants are holders of the Monégasque passport; the enclave is so tiny—under 2 sq km in area, less than a square mile—that it's hard to conceive how they all fit in. A fifth of the landmass has been reclaimed from the sea, and the coruscation of buildings barnacled on the cliffside have 30 storeys or more. Its urban planning is astounding, with roads tunnelling under the rock and sweeping round the buildings in great hairpin bends, and the railway station hidden away within the cliffside. Lifts are strategically placed to carry you swiftly from one level to another. Real estate prices are out of this world.

Royal Palace

The original old fortified town and Prince Rainier's palace sit on top of a rock, between the two harbours. At the base of the rock is Place d'Armes, where the Condamine market is held every morning. From here, take Rampe Major up to the Place du Palais, 60 m (197 ft) above sea level. If the prince is in residence, you'll see a flag flying from Sainte-Marie tower. Crowds of visitors congregate here daily to watch the Changing of the Guard, which takes place at 11.55 a.m. precisely. The palace is open for visits from June to October; guided tours only. A balcony gives you a good view of the magnificent frescoed main courtyard, dating from the 16th century. Guides lead troops of tourists from room to room, but the commentary is recorded, and there isn't really enough time to take in at leisure the vast number of opulent furnishings, landscapes, royal portraits and objets d'art on view in the grand apartments and the throne room, which are the only parts of the palace open to the public.

From the square you can look out over the port and spankingly clean industrial district of Fontvieille, and the spectacular football stadium, Stade Louis II.

Old Town

The old town is tiny but the streets and squares are full of charm. Here and there are sculptures, part of a "*chemin des arts*" (art trail), and as you stroll around you will no doubt come across the Chapelle de la Miséricorde (1639), the Musée du Vieux Monaco (historical tableaux illustrating the Grimaldi dynasty) and the Musée de la Chapelle de la Visitation, with a collection of sacred art. The neo-Romanesque Cathédrale de l'Immaculée-Conception (1875) contains the tombs of the princes of Monaco, including that of Princess Grace, which is always covered in fresh flowers. There are several superb altarpieces, some by Louis Bréa.

Musée Océanographique

Past the Jardins Saint-Martin, you'll see the palatial façade of the Museum of Oceanography, on the edge of the rock above the sea. Internationally renowned, it was built at the instigation of Prince Albert I, who was interested in all things marine. For several decades, it served as base camp for the famous Commandant Jacques Cousteau. The aquarium, in the basement, contains Mediterranean species in one section and coralline in another, the two separated by a shark lagoon. On the upper floors, the fine galleries display objects linked to maritime history and specimens collected from all the oceans of the world.

HOODWINKED

A desirable piece of property, Monaco was colonized by Phoenicians, Greeks and Romans. It came into the hands of the Grimaldis of Genoa in the 13th century, when Italy was in the throes of hostilities between the Ghibellines (partisans of the emperor) and the Guelphs (partisans of the Pope, and in favour of independence for the towns). Expelled from Genoa, the Guelf François Grimaldi sneaked his way into Ghibelline Monaco in 1297, disguised in the habit of a Franciscan monk. With the help of a band of comrades-at-arms, he took possession of the rock. The Grimaldis' sovereignty was confirmed in 1308 and recognized by France in 1512.

Monte-Carlo

When you can tear your eyes away from the fabulous yachts at anchor in Port de la Condamine, head into Monte-Carlo, the district east of the port. Monte-Carlo came into its own in 1866 with the first gaming rooms. They were so successful (and profitable) that after only three years of exploitation, Prince Charles III abolished income tax for all the Monégasques! Set in lush terraced gardens, the sumptuous Casino was designed by Charles Garnier, also responsible for the Opéra Garnier in Paris. Not to be outdone, the casino has its own opera, resplendent in velvet and gilt. You can see it on a guided tour, which also takes in the games rooms, each one more splendid than the last, with glittering chandeliers, baroque stucco work, charming frescoes and a hushed atmosphere around the

Monaco stands on ceremony: every day at 11.55 a.m., the Changing of the Guard draws crowds of onlookers.

gaming tables where players nonchalantly gamble away their fortunes. All the croupiers are of Monégasque nationality.

Opposite the casino, the Hôtel de Paris is surrounded in an aura of Belle Epoque refinement.

To the east, the Musée National occupies a beautiful turn-of-the-century villa, also designed by Charles Garnier. It has a a large collection of dolls and automatons, the oldest dating back to the 18th century. Along the sea front is the Grimaldi Forum, with conference centre, adaptable spaces for trade fairs, concert halls and auditoria. You see only the glass tip of this iceberg, which descends several storeys below the sea. Further along is Larvotto's sandy beach.

Jardin Exotique

Up on the heights, on the cliff-side, the Exotic Garden is planted in terraces with the biggest collection of cacti in Europe. At the bottom of the garden, you can enter the Grotte de l'Observatoire: a staircase leads 54 m (177 ft) underground to a large cave full of wonderful stalagmites, stalactites and other formations draped like curtains. The garden also contains the Musée d'Anthropologie préhistorique, founded by Albert I in 1902.

Cultural Notes

Architecture

The oldest surviving monuments in Provence date back to Roman times: their amphitheatres, theatres, triumphal arches, baths and bridges were built on the same lines as those of the Imperial capital. In the early Christian era, the architects adapted the Roman style for their columns and capitals; a few chapels have survived, as well as several fine octagonal baptisteries. Romanesque arrived fairly late in Provence, in the 12th century. It is also inspired by the simple lines of Roman architecture. This was the glorious era of the Cisterian monasteries and their magnificent cloisters. The Gothic style was also late reaching Provence, not until the 14th century. The best example is the Palais des Papes in Avignon. The Renaissance style hardly affected the region, except when medieval castles and forts were renovated. But baroque spread everywhere, in both religious buildings (chapels, high altars) and secular (*hôtels particuliers*—private mansions). Many official buildings were designed in neoclassical style, then, in the 19th century, neo-Byzantine, as demonstrated by the basilica of Notre-Dame-de-la-Garde that keeps watch over Marseille. Soon afterwards, people began to build villas, casinos and hotels in the fashion of the moment: neo-Moorish *(néo-mauresque)*, Belle Epoque and Art Deco.

Cistercians

The Cistercian Order was founded in 1098 at the Abbey of Cîteaux by its first abbot, Robert de Molesme (sanctified Saint Robert). It became more widespread in the following century under the guidance of Saint Bernard, the founder of Clairvaux Abbey. Taking advantage of an increasing moral role, to the detriment of the Benedictines of Cluny, the Cistercians built monasteries all over Europe, almost 700 during the Middle Ages, including Sénanque, Silvacane and Le Thoronet in Provence. Plain and functional in design, the buildings can hardly be described as frivolous, but here and there a detail belies the norm: a daring bell tower, fancifully carved capitals on the cloister columns, and so on.

The harsh life of the Cistercians, governed by the strict rule of Saint Benoît (6th century) was devoted to continual prayer, the seven daily offices interspersed with meditation and work in the fields. In order to concentrate on his duties, each monk took a vow of silence. Even today, at Sénanque, the monks communicate by written messages which they post to each other. The rules have been relaxed a little since medieval days: the monasteries have central heating, albeit barely noticeable, and the monks can sleep in till 4.10 a.m. (wake-up time varied with the seasons between 1.30 and 4.30 a.m. in the Middle Ages).

Painting Provence

Artists began to appreciate the quality of the light in Provence in the late 19th century. Monet and Renoir came in 1883, Van Gogh was dazzled by the luminosity of Arles in 1888 and persuaded Gauguin to join him. Paul Cézanne was born in Aix-en-Provence; his favourite subject was the Montagne Sainte-Victoire which he painted more than 60 times. The Impressionists and Pointillistes discovered the splendour of Saint-Tropez: first Signac, then Henri-Edmond Cross, Manguin and the Marseillais Charles Camoin. The Fauvists adored the bright sunny colours: Matisse and Dufy at Nice, Van Dongen at Monaco. From 1906 to 1908, L'Estaque on the outskirts of Marseille became the haunt of Cubists, first and foremost Braque and Picasso, who then moved to Vallauris, Cannes and Mougins, ending his days on the slopes of Sainte-Victoire. At the beginning of World War II, a number of artists found refuge in free Provence, like the surrealist Max Ernst. Others spend their last years here: Fernand Léger at Biot, Nicolas de Staël at Antibes, Chagall at Saint-Paul-de-Vence, and of course Cocteau, very active in the region. More recently, a group of New Realists found fame in Nice, with the Marseillais César, Arman, who lived in Vence, and in Nice around César, born in Marseille, Arman and Yves Klein, both born in Nice.

Perfume

The absolute essence for perfume can be obtained in several different ways: by distillation; by extraction with a solvent; by mechanical means (with a press or centrifuge), or by a technique known as *enfleurage,* used until recent times. For this method, fragile flowers such as jasmine were spread out on grids covered with solidified grease, and renewed when their fragrance had diffused into it, every three to seven days during two months. For this process, a ton of flowers yielded only a scant litre of essence. If you consider that a perfume is composed of 50 to 100 different essences, it is easy to understand why it is so costly. In the 1920s synthetic essences were invented, and gradually natural essences have been reserved for the most exclusive perfumes. It takes many years for a "nose" to learn to differentiate 3000 different scents.

Shopping

The market stalls are brimming over with hand-made objects and gaily printed fabrics, not forgetting natural products and gastronomic specialities. Provence is renowned for its antique and second-hand markets. There are many beautiful illustrated books about Provence, and tempting cookbooks.

Crafts

Pottery, faïence, ceramics, sandstone and enamel figure among the many materials used to produce the plates, bowls, vases, jugs and decorative objects crafted in small workshops and painted by hand. Yellow, green and brown are the dominant colours.

In the region of Aubagne, look for *santons*: these hand-painted clay figurines represent all the characters and animals of the Nativity scene, together with many local characters, fishermen, farmers, shepherds and milkmaids. The art was imported from Italy in the 18th century.

Olive wood is carved into bowls large and small, cheese dishes, salad servers, bottle openers and corkscrews. The village of Biot specializes in thick, heavy, coloured glass full of bubbles. And you'll have no difficulty finding an attractive locally woven basket to carry everything home.

Perfume and Natural Products

In Grasse there are several showrooms where you can test the latest creations and decide which one best suits your personality. There's a wide range of perfumes and toiletries, beautifully packaged. At Salon-de-Provence, two family firms still produce *savon de Marseille*, with 72% of natural oils, according to the century-old recipe, but it's more for heavy duty washing than bathing in luxurious foam. In boutiques and on the markets, you'll find packets of pot-pourri and dried lavender to freshen rooms and cupboards, perfumed candles, and table sets made from Provençal fabrics.

Gourmet Gifts

All the products of the olive tree, honey, cheese, nougat, candied fruit, *calissons* from Aix, *berlingots* from Carpentras, pots of *fleur de sel*—hand-picked flakes of salt from the Camargue salt marshes—delicious on a steak.

Dining Out

Considering the luscious sun-ripened fruit and vegetables, it is hardly surprising that the cuisine of Provence is hearty, colourful and healthy. This is simple, inspired country cooking, with the freshest ingredients, lots of herbs and garlic, and masses of olive oil. The Provençaux like to eat outside, but in a leafy arbour: they prefer the sun in winter, and the shade in summer.

Snacks

There are plenty of street stalls where you can buy a *jambon-beurre* (ham sandwich), an Italian-style hot *panini* or a *croque-monsieur* (toasted ham and cheese sandwich). A *pan bagnat* is a whole lunch in a bun: a large round flat bread roll filled with lettuce, slices of tomato, onion and hard-boiled egg, tuna, anchovies and olives, drizzled in olive oil and wrapped up in aluminium foil for a while to let the flavours mingle. *Fougasse* is a kind of flat bread sprinkled with salt, rosemary and olive oil or split through the middle and stuffed with ham or cheese; *pissaladière* is a pizza base topped with a thick layer of fried onion, criss-crossed with anchovy fillets and dotted with black olives.

Appetizers

The Provençal apéritif par excellence is *pastis*, an aniseed-flavoured liquid diluted with ice-cold water. With it come roast peppers in oil, tiny grey shrimp *(crevettes grises)*, or olives. *Petits gris* are little garden snails. *Poutargue*, like a grey sausage, is actually dried fish roe preserved in a wax casing. You grate it like hard cheese and eat it on bread.

Then the hors-d'oeuvres: *supions* (small squid), *châtaignes de mer* (sea urchins) especially on the Côte Bleue, *charcuterie* such as *pâté*, *rillettes* or thin slices of *saucisson*, or *beignets de courgette* (courgette fritters). Courgette flowers also make excellent fritters. The bean soup known as *soupe au pistou* owes its flavour to a purée of parmesan, garlic and basil. You can start a meal with salad—lettuce *(salade verte)*, tomato with mozzarella or mixed *(salade mêlée)*. *Salade niçoise* comprises lettuce, green beans, potatoes, tuna, anchovies, tomatoes, peppers and olives.

Fish and Seafood

Out of the Med and into the pan: *loup* (sea bass) is delicious grilled and flavoured with fennel. Other common fish are *rouget* (red mullet), *saint-pierre* (John Dory), *daurade royale* (sea bream) and sardines, stuffed or opened flat, fried or grilled. The famous *bouillabaisse* was originally a simple fishermen's dish made with damaged, unsaleable fish. There are so many versions that a charter has been set down to define its ingredients: scorpion fish, monkfish, conger eel, red mullet, onions, leeks, tomatoes, fennel, garlic, thyme, bay leaves, saffron, savory, sage, orange zest, olive oil and white wine! It is served with *croûtons* and *rouille*, an orange-red mayonnaise spiced with chilli. *Bourride* is a simplified version of bouillabaisse. Another typical Marseillais dish is *le grand ailloli*, a stew of salt cod and vegetables accompanied by a thick garlic mayonnaise. *Brandade de morue* is also made from salt cod, soaked for hours and mashed into a purée with potatoes, garlic, olive oil and cream.

Octopus is usually sliced up and grilled. Among the wide variety of seafood are *langoustes* (crayfish), *moules* (mussels), *oursins* (sea urchins) and *palourdes* (clams). There are many other shellfish that you will not recognize, such as *tellines* and *violets* but you may as well have a try. In the Rhône Valley, fricasseed eel *(anguille)* is a favourite.

Meat

In this region, the meat comes from animals raised on arid land: mutton *(mouton)*, kid *(chevreau)*, wild boar *(sanglier)* and rabbit *(lapin)*. There is some beef: a typical Sunday dish in the Camargue is a daube using meat from the bull *(toro)*, served with raviolis. *Lou piech* is veal stuffed with chard, peas, beans, grated courgettes, egg and Parmesan cheese. In *pieds et paquets* the *pieds* are lamb's feet and the *paquets* are parcels made from squares of sheep's stomach wrapped round pieces of salt pork or meat stuffing, all simmered together for five or six hours in a tasty sauce.

Vegetables

A whole range of vegetables is used to accompany these dishes: asparagus *(asperges)*, baby artichokes *(poivrade)*, sweet peppers *(poivrons)*, tomatoes, courgettes, aubergines, onions, fennel *(fenouil)* and chard *(blettes)*. Cardoons *(cardons)* are served with a hot dipping sauce made of oil and anchovies. Tomatoes, courgettes, aubergines, onions and peppers, cut into small pieces and stewed in oil, make ratatouille, which can be eaten hot or cold, as an hors d'œuvre or with your main dish.

You may not be able to identify them, but don't be afraid to taste.

Desserts

Melons, figs, apricots, peaches, strawberries, plums, persimmons *(kakis)*—fruit is the basis of most desserts: in tarts, compotes, jams, gratins, crumbles, sorbets and ice cream. Not forgetting *crème caramel*, *mousse au chocolat*, *îles flottantes* (poached meringue islands floating in an egg custard sea). *Riz au lait* is rice pudding, while *gâteau de riz* is a more solid version, eaten cold and coated with caramel sauce.

Drinks

There's nothing to stop you drinking beer—the French and Belgian makes are very refreshing, but don't forget that this is a wine-growing region. From the Côtes du Rhône to the wines of Bandol, from the Côtes du Luberon to the Côteaux de Provence, there is plenty to choose from. The red wines are the the most esteemed, particularly Châteauneuf-du-Pape, or Château-Vignelaure, from the Côteaux-d'Aix. The numerous *vins rosés* are fresh and perfect with a light meal. The whites tend to be dry.

Most people end their meal with a coffee *(café)*, black and strong in a small cup. For a double size, ask for *un grand café*. Tea *(thé)* is increasingly popular (served weak).

Sports

This is outdoors country and you can practise almost any kind of sport—hiking, cycling, horse-riding, rock climbing, hang-gliding, kayaking, golf. Water sports are naturally foremost on the Côte d'Azur, but also on the lakes and waterways further inland.

Water sports

The Mediterranean resorts offer a tremendous variety of activities. Windsurfing is incontestably one of the leading sports, and the most popular places for practising it are the Beau-Rivage beach at Saint-Raphaël, at L'Almanarre near Hyères and at the far end of the tombolo on the Giens peninsula. World Cup competitions are held every year at L'Almanarre. In most resorts you can hire jet-skis, or go water skiing, sailing, deep-sea fishing or diving—there are centres all along the coast.

Some of the best spots for diving are the Giens peninsula and the Iles d'Hyères. At Port-Cros in particular, you will never forget the corals and gardens of sea grasses, and the groupers are not shy at all. If you just want to swim, the water is clear, clean and warm, though if you want a sandy beach, you're more likely to find it at the foot of the Massif des Maures.

Cycling

Every year, thousands of cyclists pedal along twisting minor roads of Provence, a region that's ideal for tours of a few hours or a few days. If the passes of the Côte d'Azur seem too daunting, then head for the Camargue and the Digue à la Mer skirting the marshes and the Mediterranean, or the bucolic Luberon, where the roads are hilly but not too steep. A marked trail, "Le Luberon en vélo" (The Luberon by Bike) guides you from Cavaillon to Forcalquier in 100 km (60 miles) of secondary roads and byways. If you're feeling ambitious, you might like to tackle some of the stages of the Tour de France, Mont Ventoux being one of the favourites, and one of the most arduous.

Hiking

Whatever your destination, don't forget your walking boots. On the Côte d'Azur, you can still hike along the old Sentier des Douaniers (Excisemen's Path) along parts of the shore; the most attractive stretches are between Les Lecques and Bandol and around Cap Lardier and Cap Camarat near Saint-Tropez. In summer, the Massif des Maures and L'Esterel are often closed because of the risk of forest fires, but when they are open, they provide infinite sources of adventure, as are Sainte-Victoire and Cap Bénat near Le Lavandou. Further west, the GR 98 trail, very well-trodden in summer, links all the *calanques* between Callelongue south of Marseille and Cassis.

In Provence, there are numerous trails in the Luberon and through the Gorges du Verdon, notably the Sentier Martel, which has some dizzying stretches along its 14-km (9 mile) length. You can walk through the cedar forests or the ochre quarries of Roussillon and Rustrel, or make longer hikes on the trails of the Grande Randonnée (GR 6, 9 and 97) criss-crossing the region.

Other sports

Rock climbing is practised on the Dentelles de Montmirail, in the calanques at Marseille (particularly at En-Vau) or in the Gorges du Verdon. This last is also an ideal location for canyoning, kayaking and rafting. However, be aware that the section below Point Sublime is reserved for experienced devotees only. Beginners should head for the lower Verdon, downriver from Sainte-Croix lake. This is also a good area for hang-gliding, a sport that is also practised on the Côte d'Azur, especially from Mont Gros near Roquebrune. Horse-riding is popular everywhere, but especially in the Camargue, on farms and around Saintes-Maries de-la-Mer.

Some of France's finest golf courses are in this region. The Golf de Mougins in Cannes is a once in a lifetime experience. Other recommended courses are at Sainte Maxime, Saint-Andréol and the delightful Golf de Servannes in the Alpilles.

The Hard Facts

Airports

Two international airports serve the region: Marseille and Nice, which is the second-largest in France and built on a spectacular site almost in the sea. The entire eastern wall is glass, and you can gaze at the city and bay while you wait for your flight. Internal flights link Paris with Avignon, Nîmes and Toulon. A very efficient helicopter service links Nice and Monaco.

Climate

The Côte d'Azur enjoys a typical Mediterranean climate. Winters are mild: in January the temperature averages 11°C (52°F) in Menton. Summers are dry and sunny; the heat is tempered to a certain extent by the wind. The stretch from Beaulieu-sur-Mer to Menton is the mildest, and temperatures rarely drop below zero. All year long, but particularly in spring and autumn, the western Côte d'Azur and Provence are swept by the chilly mistral wind, which can reach a speed of over 100 kph (60 mph). Its one advantage is that it blows away the clouds, the sky is blue and the landscape clear.

Usually, rain falls mainly at the end of autumn and beginning of winter. Sea temperatures are around 15°C (60°F) in April, 20°C (68°F) in June and as high as 24°C (75°F) in August.

Communications

The postal service is is run by La Poste. Letterboxes are yellow, with a blue stylized bird.

You can make international calls from any callbox, using phone cards which exist in 50 or 120 units and are sold in post offices and tobacconists. Calls to other European countries are cheaper after 7 p.m. on weekdays, on Saturday afternoons and all day on Sunday. If you are placing a call within France, you need only the ten-digit number of your contact (beginning with 0). To make an international call, dial 00 then the country code (1 for US and Canada, 44 for the UK, the area code (minus initial zero) and the local number. Faxes can be sent from most hotels and post offices. Some post offices have Internet access, and there are Internet cafés in some towns. Many large hotels can also provide Internet access.

Driving

It is very easy to hire a car from one of the big international companies. In general drivers must be over 21, sometimes 25, and have held a licence for more than a year.

On the motorways, the speed limit is 130 kph (80 mph), reduced to 110 kph (68 mph) in wet weather. In towns and villages the limit is 50 kph (31 mph) and elsewhere 90 kph (55 mph), or 80 kph (50 mph) in wet weather. The wearing of seat belts is compulsory in both front and rear seats. In town, do not use the lanes reserved for buses and taxis. And don't forget to feed the numerous and often expensive parking meters and pay-and-display machines: the traffic warden will not be far away!

Medieval villages were not designed for cars, and parking is often a problem in summer when hordes of sightseers descend on them. When you drive up, you will probably be waved into a distant field by a gendarme (or someone who does not look the slightest bit like a gendarme) and have to walk the rest of the way.

Electricity

220 volts, 50 Hz, plugs with two round pins. Take an adapter.

Emergencies

In a medical emergency, telephone 15 for the SAMU (ambulance service). To call the police dial 17 and for the fire service 18.

Essentials

Whatever the season, have your swimming costume, sunglasses and sunhat to hand. Take light clothing, preferably cotton, and a sweater for the cool evenings or windy days. If you are planning on some walking, good shoes will be useful, as will plastic sandals or diving slippers for the many pebbled beaches and the rocky depths. In summer you will be very glad of an insect repellent.

Formalities

You need a valid passport or identity card to enter the country. Visitors coming from the UK or other EU countries, 17 years or older, may import the following goods, not purchased tax free: 200 cigarettes or 50 cigars or 250 g tobacco, 1 litre spirits over 22° or 2 litres of spirits of less than 22° and 2 litres of non-sparkling wine, 250 ml eau de toilette and 50 g perfume. The quantities are the same for visitors of non-EU countries but they can buy their goods tax-free.

Health

Apart from too much sun and too much food and drink, there is little risk to health and you need no particular vaccinations. In summer, remember to apply your sun-block and wear a hat and sunglasses. If you are on medication, take supplies with you as the same brands and dosages are not always available. France and the UK have a reciprocal health agreement; before you leave home, apply for a form E111 (from your local post office) in case you have to consult a doctor.

Markets

Most towns have at least one market day a week. The following are special, seasonal markets.
Aix en Provence: bric-à-brac Saturday mornings, crafts in July and August, *santons* in December
Antibes: clothing every moning except Monday
Apt: pottery in August
Aubagne: bric-à-brac last Sunday of month, *santons* December
Avignon: bric-à-brac Saturday and Sunday mornings, crafts in July
Cagnes sur Mer: clothing every morning Tuesday to Friday
Carpentras: truffle market Friday morning November to March
Cassis: *santons* in December
Cavaillon: crafts second fortnight in August
Gordes: pottery in July
Isle sur Sorge: bric-à-brac every Saturday, Sunday, Monday (flea market Sundays)
Marseille: bric-à-brac second Sunday of the month; garlic market end June, early July; *santons* in December
Vence: clothing and food Tuesdays and Fridays
Villeneuve-les-Avignon: bric-à-brac Saturday morning.

Media

Large hotels have cable or satellite TV so you can watch the news in English from CNN, Sky or BBC World. English newspapers are widely available in all the seaside resorts of the Riviera. The choice is much reduced in the interior.

Money

The Euro is issued in notes of 5, 10, 20, 100, 200 and 500 Euros and coins of 1, 2, 5, 10, 20 and 50 centimes and 1 and 2 Euros. Credit cards, Visa and Mastercard preferably, are widely accepted except in a few small hotels and restaurants. Your card can also be used to obtain cash from ATMs, provided you know your PIN number. Travellers cheques are generally accepted.

Opening Hours

As a general rule, shops and boutiques are open Tuesday to Saturday from 9 or 9.30 a.m. to 6, 6.30 or 7 p.m. Sometimes they also open on Monday afternoons. Shops are closed on Sundays with the exception of some food stores. In villages and small towns, most shops close for two or three hours at lunchtime. That being said, shops of all kinds keep longer hours in summer.

Museums are almost all closed on Mondays, sometimes on Tuesdays. Some keep restricted hours or close completely out of season. When you arrive in a town, call in at the tourist office to check on hours, as many museums are undergoing renovation.

Photography
All types of film are available at reasonable prices. Many shops can develop and print your photographs in an hour. Make allowance for the bright Mediterranean light (use a polarizing filter, for example).

Public Holidays

January 1	New Year's Day
March-April	Easter Monday
May 1	Labour Day
May 8	Armistice 1945
May-June	Ascension Day
June	Whit Monday
July 14	Bastille Day
August 15	Assumption
November 1	Armistice 1918
December 25	Christmas Day

Security
Take great care with your belongings. Never leave them unguarded at the beach, and make sure everything is out of sight in your car, and all the doors locked. Most hotels have a safe at reception or in the rooms where you can leave your valuables while you go out sightseeing.

Tipping
Service is always included, but nevertheless it is customary to tip waiters and taxi drivers.

Tourist Offices
In every city the tourist offices (Maison de la France) are well equipped with brochures and maps. Ask here for a calendar of cultural events and for information on guided tours. They will also have up-to-date information on opening hours and market days. The Syndicats d'Initiative are local offices, and may be able to help you find accommodation.

Toilets
Called *toilettes, cabinets* or WC, public toilets can be found at some beaches and in bars, museums and hotels, and at the motorway *stations-service*, where there are generally facilities for changing and feeding babies. Men is *Hommes* and Ladies *Femmes*.

Trains
The TGV Méditerranée links Paris with Marseille in 3 hours. It takes about 7 or 8 hours by Eurostar and TGV from London to Marseille. Beyond Marseille, the trains are slower (almost 3 hours more to reach Nice). Locally, it is better to rent a car, but you can relax on the branch lines of the SNCF along the coast, or use buses in the interior.

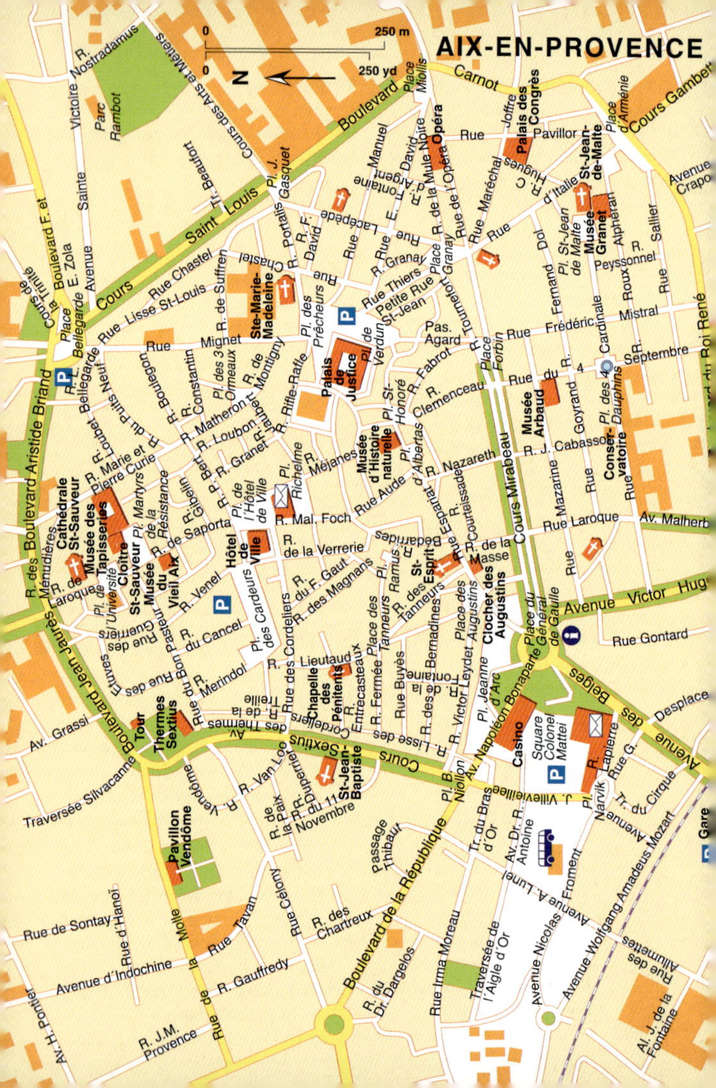
AIX-EN-PROVENCE
0
250 m
0
250 yd
N
Parc Rambot
R. Nostradamus
Cours des Arts et Métiers
Boulevard Carnot
Place Miollis
Cours Saint Louis
Pl. J. Gasquet
Opéra
Palais des Congrès
Rue Pavillon
Joffre
St-Jean-de-Malte
Musée Granet
Place d'Arménie
Cours Gambetta
Avenue Crapone
Rue Manuel
Rue Lacépède
Rue Fontaine d'Argent
R. David
R. de la Mule Noire
Rue de l'Opéra
Rue Maréchal
R. C. Hugues
Rue d'Italie
Pl. St-Jean de Malte
R. Peyssonnel
Roux Alphéran
R. Sallier
Boulevard F. et E. Zola
Cours de la Trinité
Avenue Sainte Victoire
Tr. Beaufort
Rue Chastel
Rue Lisse St-Louis
R. de Suffren
Ste-Marie-Madeleine
R. Portalis
R. F. David
Rue E. Fontaine
R. Granet
Rue Thiers
Petite Rue St-Jean
Place Granet
Tournefort
Place Bellegarde
Rue Mignet
Pl. des Prêcheurs
Palais de Justice
Pl. de Verdun
Pas. Agard
R. Fabrot
Place Forbin
Rue Frédéric Mistral
Fernand Dol
Cardinale
R. 4 Septembre
Rue du Roi René
Boulevard Aristide Briand
R. L. Bellegarde
R. du Puits Neuf
R. Boulegon
R. Constantin
Pl. des 3 Ormeaux
R. de Montigny
R. Rifle-Rafle
R. Matheron
R. Loubon
R. Jaubert
Pl. St. Honoré
R. Clemenceau
Rue du 4
Musée Arbaud
Goyrand
Pl. des 4 Dauphins
R. Lobet
R. Marie et Pierre Curie
Pl. Martyrs de la Résistance
R. Gibelin
R. Bert
R. P. Granet
Pl. Richelme
R. Méjanes
Musée d'Histoire naturelle
Pl. d'Albertas
R. Nazareth
R. J. Cabassol
Conservatoire
Rue Mazarine
Cathédrale St-Sauveur
Musée des Tapisseries
Cloître St-Sauveur
Musée du Vieil Aix
R. de Saporta
Pl. de l'Hôtel de Ville
R. Mal. Foch
Rue Aude
Rue Espariat
R. Courteissade
Cours Mirabeau
Rue Laroque
Av. Malherbe
R. des Ménudières
R. de Laroque
Pl. de l'Université
Hôtel de Ville
R. de la Verrerie
R. Bédarrides
R. de la Masse
Clocher des Augustins
R. Venel
R. du F. Gaut
R. des Magnans
Pl. Ramus
R. des Tanneurs
St-Esprit
Avenue Victor Hugo
Rue des Guerriers
R. du Cancel
Pl. des Cardeurs
Rue des Cordeliers
Place des Tanneurs
R. des Bernardines
Place des Augustins
Place du Général de Gaulle
Rue Gontard
Boulevard Jean Jaurès
Rue des Étuves
Rue du Bon Pasteur
R. Mérindol
R. Lieutaud
Chapelle des Pénitents
R. Entrecasteaux
R. Fermée
Rue Buyès
R. de la Fontaine
T. R. de la Fontaine
R. Leydet
Victor
Pl. Jeanne d'Arc
Rue des Belges
Avenue des Belges
Desplace
Av. Grassi
Tour
Thermes Sextius
Av. des Thermes
T. R. de la Treille
Cordeliers
R. Lisse des Cordeliers
Cours Sextius
St-Jean-Baptiste
Av. Napoléon Bonaparte
Casino
Square Colonel Mattei
R. Lapierre
Rue G. Desplace
Traversée Silvacanne
R. Vendôme
R. Van Loo
R. Dupertier
R. de la Paix
R. du 11 Novembre
Pl. B. Niollon
J. Villevieille
Pl. Narvik
Tr. du Cirque
Gare
Pavillon Vendôme
passage Thibaud
Tr. du Bras d'Or
Av. Dr. R. Antoine
Avenue A. Lunel
Froment
Avenue Wolfgang Amadeus Mozart
Rue de Sontay
Rue d'Hanoï
Rue de la Molle
Rue Tavan
Rue Célony
R. des Chartreux
Boulevard de la République
Rue Irma Moreau
Traversée de l'Aigle d'Or
Avenue Nicolas
Avenue Wolfgang
Rue des Allumettes
Avenue d'Indochine
R. Gauffredy
R. du Dr. Dargelos
Av. H. Pontier
R. J.M. Provence
Al. J. de la Fontaine

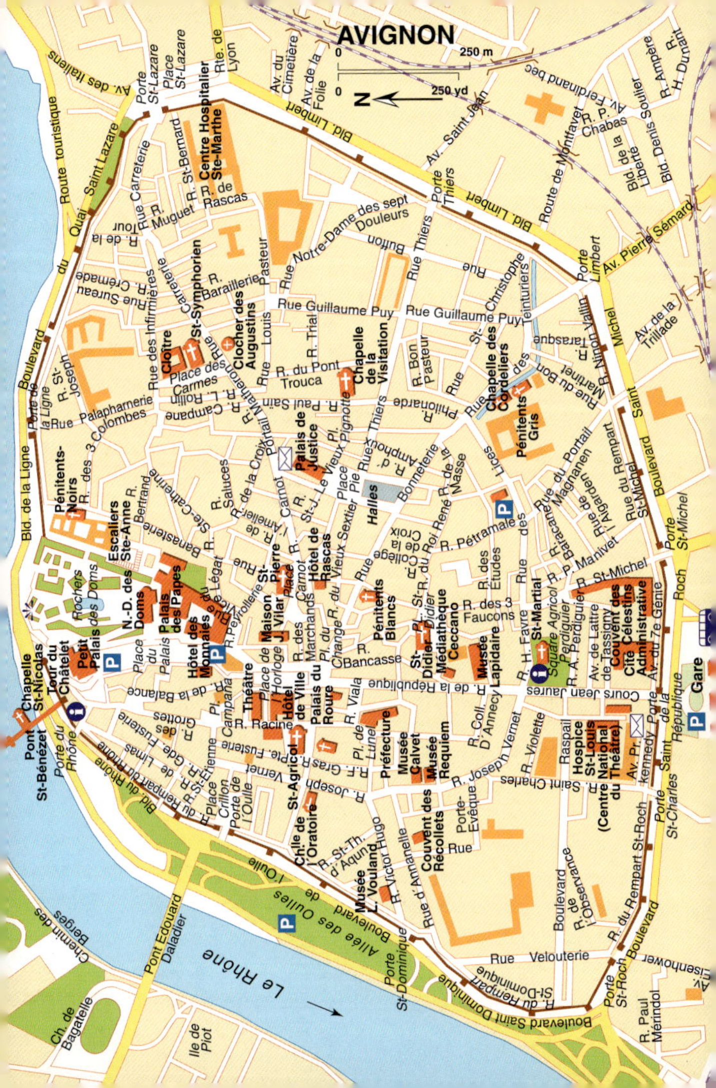
AVIGNON
0
250 m
0
250 yd
N
Le Rhône
Pont St-Bénézet
Chapelle St-Nicolas
Tour du Châtelet
Petit Palais
N.-D. des Doms
Rochers des Doms
Palais des Papes
Hôtel des Monnaies
Place du Palais
Escaliers Ste-Anne
Pénitents-Noirs
Cloître
St-Symphorien
Place des Carmes
Clocher des Augustins
Centre Hospitalier Ste-Marthe
Chapelle de la Visitation
Palais de Justice
Halles
Place Pie
Chapelle des Cordeliers
Pénitents Gris
Maison J. Vilar
St-Pierre
Hôtel de Rascas
Pénitents Blancs
St-Didier
Médiathèque Ceccano
Musée Lapidaire
St-Martial
Square Agricol Perdiguier
Couvent des Célestins
Cité Administrative
Théâtre
Place de l'Horloge
Hôtel de Ville
Palais du Roure
Préfecture
Musée Calvet
Musée Requiem
St-Agricol
Ch.lle de l'Oratoire
Musée L. Vouland
Couvent des Récollets
Hospice St-Louis (Centre National du Théâtre)
Gare
Porte de la République
Porte St-Charles
Porte St-Roch
Porte St-Dominique
Porte de l'Oulle
Porte du Rhône
Porte de la Ligne
Porte St-Lazare
Porte Thiers
Porte Limbert
Porte St-Michel
Place St-Lazare
Place Crillon
Place Campana
Pont Edouard Daladier
Ile de Piot
Ch. de Bagatelle
Chemin des Berges
Allée des Oulles
Boulevard de l'Oulle
Boulevard Saint Dominique
Boulevard Saint Roch
Boulevard Saint Michel
Boulevard de la Ligne
Bld. de la Ligne
Quai Saint Lazare
Route touristique
Av. des Italiens
Rte. de Lyon
Av. du Cimetière
Av. de la Folie
Bld. Limbert
Av. Saint Jean
Av. Ferdinand Bec
R. P. Chabas
Bld. de la Liberté
Bld. Denis Soulier
R. Ampère
R. H. Dunant
Route de Montfavet
Av. Pierre Sémard
Av. de la Trillade
Av. Eisenhower
R. Paul Mérindol
Rue Carreterie
R. St-Bernard
R. de Rascas
R. Muguet
R. de la Tour
R. Crémade
Rue Sureau
Rue des Infirmières
R. Carreterie
R. Barailleries
Rue Pasteur
Rue Notre-Dame des sept Douleurs
Rue Buffon
Rue Thiers
Rue Guillaume Puy
Rue Louis
R. Trial
R. du Pont Trouca
R. Bon Pasteur
Rue St-Christophe
Rue des Teinturiers
R. de Tarasque
R. Martinet
Rue du Bon
R. Ninon Vallin
R. St-Joseph
Rue Palapharnerie
R. des 3 Colombes
R. L. Rollin
R. Campane
R. Matheron
Rue Portail Matheron
R. de la Croix
R. Paul Saïn
Rue Philonarde
R. d'Amphoux
R. Bonneterie
R. de la Masse
Rue Carnot
Pl. Pignotte
Pl. St-J. Le Vieux
Rue du Vieux Sextier
R. Saluces
R. Bertrand
R. Ste-Catherine
R. Banasterie
R. de l'Amelier
R. Pétramale
R. Collège de la Croix
R. du Roi René
R. des Études
Rue des Lices
Rue du Portail Magnanen
Rue de l'Aigarden
Rue du Rempart St-Michel
R. Barcane
R. P. Manivet
R. St-Michel
R. Peyrollerie
R. du Vice Légat
R. des Marchands
Pl. du Change
R. du Change
R. Bancasse
R. St-Didier
R. des 3 Faucons
R. H. Favre
R. Agricol Perdiguier
Av. de Lattre de Tassigny
Av. du 7e Génie
R. de la Balance
R. de la République
Cours Jean Jaurès
R. des Grottes
R. Racine
R. Viala
Pl. de Lunel
R. Coll. D'Annecy
R. Violette
Raspail
R. Gde. Fusterie
R. Pte. Fusterie
R. F. Gras
R. de Limas
R. du Rempart du Rhône
Bld. du Rhône
R. St-Etienne
R. Joseph Vernet
R. Saint Charles
Av. Pr. Kennedy
R. St-Th. d'Aquin
R. Victor Hugo
Rue d'Annanelle
Porte Évêque
Rue Velouterie
Boulevard de l'Observance
R. du Rempart St-Roch
R. du Rempart St-Dominique

MARSEILLE
0
500 m
500 yd
Corse
N
Digue Sainte-Marie
Quai Jean Charcot
Gare maritime
Bassin de la Grande Joliette
Gare maritime
Digue du Fort St-Jean
Calanques Château d´If
Palais des Congrès
Jardin du Pharo
Fort Saint-Jean
Quai M. Pagnol
Bas-Fort St-Nicolas
Bld. Charles Livon
Fort d´Entrecasteaux
Fort St-Nicolas
Rampe St-Maurice
R. E. Duchêne
Av. de la Corse
St-Victor
ST-VICTOR
Rue Sainte
Place St-Victor
Musée du Santon
Bassin de Carénage
Tunnel Saint-Laurent
Quai Rive Neuve
Théâtre de la Criée
Rue Neuve Ste-Catherine
R. Petit Chantier
Rue de la Croix
R. des Tyrans
Rue Rigord
Rue Robert
Rue Sain
R. Fort Notre-Dame
Cours d´Estienn
Quai Riv
P
Vieux Port
Ferry
Hôtel de Ville
HOTEL DE VILLE
Quai du port
Rue de la Loge
R. de la Prison
Maison diamantée
Musée des Docks Romains
Caisserie
Musée du Vieux Marseille
R. H. Tasso
Rue de
Av. St-Jean
R. des Martegales
Saint-Laurent
R. St-Laurent
Théâtre Grec
Esplanade de la Tourette
Av. Vaudoyer
Quai de la Tourette
R. St-Thome
R. de la Cathédrale
Place de Lenche
Rue
le Préau des Accoules
Montée des Accoules
Cloch des Accoule
R. des Moulins
R. des Muettes
Pl. des Moulins
R. du Refuge
R. Baussenque
R. Ste Françoise
Rue de l´Evêché
R. Four du Chapitre
Ancien Evêché
Place de la Major
Egl. de la Vieille Major
Cathédrale N.-D. de la Major
LE PANIER
R. Petit du Puits
R. du Panier
R. des Cord
Tour des Trinitaire
la Vieille Charité
Musé d´Archéologi
Rue de l´Evêche
Av. R. Schuman
R. Jean-François Le
Rue de Mazenod
Quai de la Joliette
Bld. d Dames

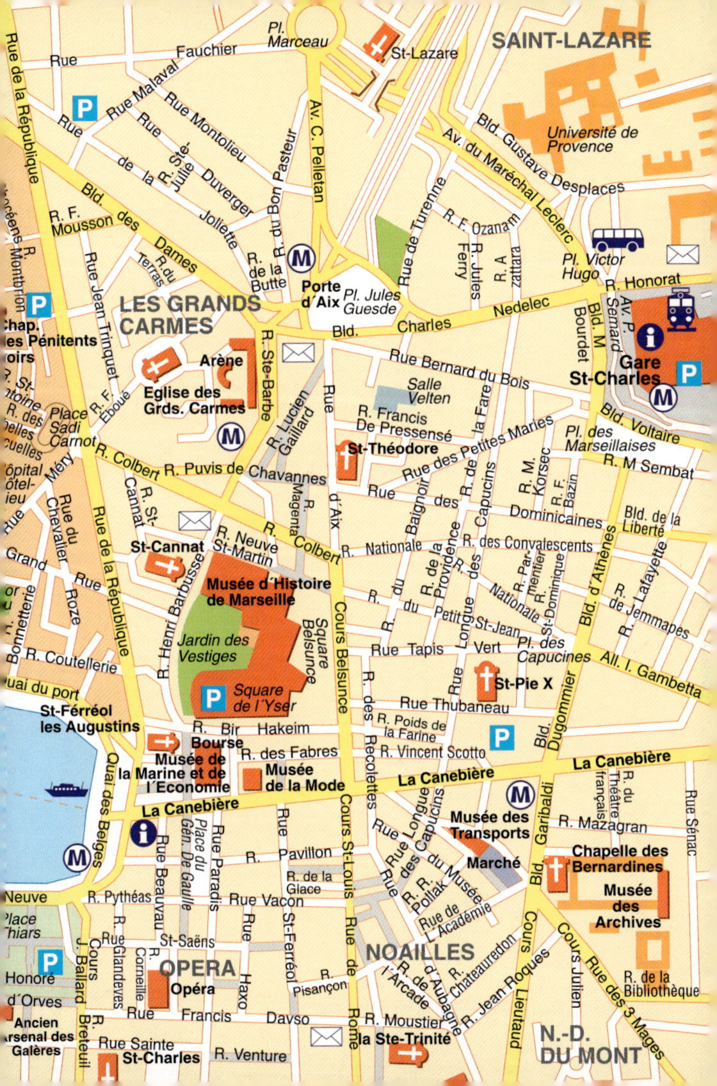

SAINT-LAZARE
Université de Provence
St-Lazare
Pl. Marceau
Rue Fauchier
Rue de la République
Rue Malaval
Rue Montolieu
Rue de la Joliette
R. Ste-Julie
Duverger
R. du Bon Pasteur
Av. C. Pelletan
Bld. Gustave Desplaces
Av. du Maréchal Leclerc
R. de Turenne
R. F. Ozanam
R. Jules Ferry
R. A zattara
Pl. Victor Hugo
R. Honorat
Bld. des Dames
R. F. Mousson
R. du Terras
R. de la Butte
Porte d'Aix
Pl. Jules Guesde
Bld. Charles Nedelec
Bld. M Bourdet
Av. P. Semard
Gare St-Charles
LES GRANDS CARMES
Rue Jean Trinquet
R. F. Eboué
Arène
Eglise des Grds. Carmes
R. Ste-Barbe
R. Lucien Gaillard
Rue d'Aix
Rue Bernard du Bois
Salle Velten
R. Francis De Pressensé
St-Théodore
Rue des Petites Maries
Bld. Voltaire
Pl. des Marseillaises
R. M Sembat
Place Sadi Carnot
R. Colbert
R. Puvis de Chavannes
R. Magenta
Rue des Dominicaines
R. Baignoir
R. de la Fare
R. des Capucins
R. M. Korsec
R. F. Bazin
Bld. de la Liberté
R. St-Cannat
St-Cannat
R. Neuve St-Martin
R. Nationale
R. des Convalescents
R. de la Providence
R. Longue des Capucins
R. Parmentier
R. St-Dominique
Bld. d'Athènes
R. Lafayette
R. de Jemmapes
Rue du Chevalier Roze
Grand Rue
R. Coutellerie
Musée d'Histoire de Marseille
R. Henri Barbusse
Jardin des Vestiges
Square Belsunce
Cours Belsunce
R. du Petit St-Jean
Rue Tapis Vert
Pl. des Capucines
All. L. Gambetta
St-Pie X
Square de l'Yser
Rue Thubaneau
R. Poids de la Farine
R. Vincent Scotto
Bld. Dugommier
Quai du port
St-Férréol les Augustins
R. Bir Hakeim
Bourse
Musée de la Marine et de l'Economie
R. des Fabres
Musée de la Mode
R. des Récolettes
La Canebière
R. du Théâtre français
Rue Sénac
Quai des Belges
Rue Beauvau
Place du Gén. De Gaulle
Rue Paradis
R. Pavillon
Cours St-Louis
Musée des Transports
R. Mazagran
Marché
Bld. Garibaldi
Chapelle des Bernardines
Musée des Archives
R. Pythéas
Rue Vacon
R. de la Glace
Rue du Musée
R. Pollak
Rue de l'Académie
Rue St-Saëns
Rue Glandeves
R. Corneille
Rue Haxo
Rue St-Ferréol
Rue de Rome
NOAILLES
R. Chateauredon
Cours Lieutaud
Cours Julien
Rue des 3 Mages
R. de la Bibliothèque
OPERA
Opéra
R. Pisançon
R. de l'Arcade
R. d'Aubagne
R. Jean Roques
Cours J. Ballard
Rue Francis Davso
R. Moustier
la Ste-Trinité
N.-D. DU MONT
R. Breteuil
Rue Sainte
St-Charles
R. Venture
Arsenal des Galères

CANNES
0
200 m
0
200 yd
N
BAIE DE CANNES
GOLFE DE LA NAPOULE
Plage de la Croisette
Bld. de la Croisette
Vieux Port
Palais des Festivals et des Congrès
Casino Municipal
Théâtre de la Mer
Esplanade G. Pompidou
Prom. Robert Fabre Le Bret
Jetée Albert Edouard
Gare maritime
La Pantiéro
Marché aux fleurs Allées de la Liberté
Pl. Général de Gaulle
N.-D. du Bon Voyage
Hôtel de Ville
Halles
Centre administratif
Quai St Pierre
Quai Max Laubeuf
Espl. Mal Leclerc
Sq. J. Hibert
Square F. Mistral
Plage du Midi
Boulevard Jean Hibert
Rue Georges Clemenceau
Le Suquet
N.-D. de Bonne Espérance
Tour de la Castre
Musée de la Castre
R. de la Castre
R. Louis Perrissol
R. du Pré
R. du Suquet
R. St-Dizier
Pl. B. Cornut Gentille
R. du Dr Gazagnaire
R. du Marché
Rue Félix Faure
R. Meynadier
R. E. Négrin
R. L. Blanc
Rue Tuby
Bld. Victor Tuby
Av. des Anciens Combattants d'Afrique du Nord
Av. Bachaga S. Boualam
Bld. de la Ferrage
R. Maréchal Joffre
R. Vénizelos
R. J. de Riouffe
Rue Buttura
R. Mal. Foch
R. du 24 Août
R. des Belges
Rue St-Honoré
Rue des Serbes
Rue Hoche
R. H. Vagliano
R. des Etats-Unis
Rue Macé
R. du Cdt André
R. Dr. R. Monod
Rue Molière
Rue Marceau
Rue Jean Jaurès
Place Gambetta
Marché
Rue d'Antibes
Bld. d'Alsace
Bld. de la République
R. St-Victor
Rue Merle
R. Haddad Simon
R. L. Braille
R. de Mimont
Pl. P. Sémard
Pl. de la Gare
Avenue St-Nicolas
Av. du Mar. Galliéni
R. de Suffren
Bld. Carnot
Pl. du 18 Juin
Av. du Petit Juas
R. H. Paschke
Avenue de Grasse
Rue L. Blanc
R. L. Pastour
Bld. Guynemer
Parc Donatien Mero
Avenue de Grasse
Pl. Stanislas
R. des Suisses
R. du Pont Romain
R. Guy de Maupassant
R. du Lac
Iles de

MONACO
0
400 m
0
400 yd.
N
Monte Carlo
Digue semi-flottante
PORT DE MONACO
LA CONDAMINE
Théâtre du Fort Antoine
Pointe de la Poudrière
Musée océanographique
Jardins St-Martin
Cathédrale
Hôtel de Ville
Palais princier
Musée
Pl. du Palais
Marché
Zoo
PORT DE FONTVIEILLE
FONTVIEILLE
Héliport
Espace de Fontvieille
Roseraie Princesse Grace
Stade Louis II
PORT DE CAP-D'AIL
Sanbarbani
Musée d'Anthropologie préhistorique
Jardin Exotique
Parc Princesse Antoinette
LES REVOIRES
France
Stade Couvert
Sacré Cœur
GARE
Ste-Dévote
St-Charles
Casino
Salle Garnier
Café de Paris
Centre de Congrès Auditorium
Grimaldi Forum, Plage
Anse du Portier
Spélugues
Allée des Boulingrins
Pl. du Casino
Millefiori
Av. Princesse Grace
Bld. du Larvotto
Av. Princesse Alice
Av. de la Madone
Av. des Spélugues
Bld. des Moulins
Bld. Princesse Charlotte
Av. de Roqueville
R. Bellevue
R. Bel Respiro
Bld. de Suisse
Av. de Monte Carlo
Bld. Louis II
Av. d'Ostende
Av. Présid. J.-F. Kennedy
Quai Albert 1er
Bld. Albert 1er
Quai Antoine 1er
Av. de la Quarantaine
Av. de la Porte Neuve
R. des Remparts
Av. des Pins
Pl. de la Visitation
Av. Saint Martin
Av. du Port
Av. Saige
R. Princesse Antoinette
R. Suffren Reymond
R. Princesse Caroline
R. de Millo
Pl. d'Armes
R. Grimaldi
Accès Ste-Dévote
R. Grimaldi Gare
Bld. Rainier III
Bd. Charles III
Accès Gare
Bld. du Jardin Exotique
Av. Pasteur
Moyenne Corniche N7
Ch. Frontière de Grima
R. Victor Hugo
R. H. Labande
R. J. Jaurès
R. Malbousquet
R. Jean
Av. Hector Otto
Ascenseur
Bld. de Belgique
Av. de l'Hermitage
Bld. du Jardin Exotique
Fontvieille
Av. Prince Héréditaire Albert
R. du Gabian
Av. des Papalins
Quai des Sanbarbani
Av. des Castelans
Av. des Guelfes
Alsace

NICE
BAIE DES ANGES
400 m
400 yd.
N
Gare de Provence
Gare Nice-Ville
Gare Riquier
Gare maritime
Stade municipal Vauban
Palais des Expositions
Centre Commercial
Acropolis
Musée d'Histoire Naturelle
Musée d'Art Moderne
Théâtre
Hôpital St-Roch
Notre-Dame
Hôtel des Postes
Musée Marc Chagall
Eglise Russe
Musée Masséna
Palais de la Méditerranée
Casino Ruhl
Théâtre de Verdure
Jardin Albert 1er
Hôtel de Ville
Opéra
Palais de Justice
Cathédrale
Palais Lascaris
St-Jacques
Vieille Ville
Cimetière
Le Château
Musée naval Tour Bellanda
Terra Amata
Port Lympia
Bassin des Amiraux
Bassin du Commerce
LYMPIA
RIQUIER
CARABACEL
CAMP LONG
LA BUFFA
ST - ÉTIENNE
Promenade des Anglais
Quai des États-Unis
Quai Rauba Capeu
Quai Lunel
Av. Jean Médecin
Av. Malausséna
Bld. Gambetta
Bld. Victor Hugo
Av. St.-Jean-Bapt.
Av. Félix Faure
Bld. Jean Jaurès
Bld. Carabacel
Bld. de Cimiez
Av. des Arènes de Cimiez
Bld. Dubouchage
Bld. Raimbaldi
Bld. de Stalingrad
Bld. Carnot
Bld. Franck Pilatte
Bld. de Riquier
Av. de la République
Esplanade Kennedy
Av. Mal Lyautey
Le Paillon
Grande Corniche, Menton
Moyenne Corniche, Monaco
Corniche Inférieure, Villefranche
Antibes, Cannes

Jardins de la Fontaine
Quai de la Fontaine
Square Antonin
Boulevard Gambetta
Maison A. Daudet
Rue de la Boucarie
Rue de l'Agau
St-Charles
Pl. St-Charles
R. Fléchier
Rue Ranqueil
R. de Bourgogne
Rue de la Vierge
R. de l'Enclos-Rey
Coupole des Halles
Halles
Place d'Assas
R. Voltaire
R. Crébillon
R. Gaston Boissier
Bld. A. Daudet
R. Molière
R. des Flottes
Rue du Grand Couvent
R. Littré
Rue Guizot
R. Corconne
Rue des Halles
R. de la Ferrage
Rue Nationale
Rue du Bât d'Argent
Rue Sigalon
Rue des Lombards
Carré d'Art
Pl. de la Maison Carrée
Maison carrée
R. Corneille
Rue Général Perrier
Rue des Orangers
Pl. de l'Esclafidous
R. Crémieux
Rue Nationale
Pl. Division Daguet
Porte d'Auguste
St-Baudile
Pl. Gabriel Péri
R. Racine
Place Questel
Boulevard Victor Hugo
R. de la Maison Carrée
Pl. de la Calade
R. de l'Horloge
Pl. de l'Horloge
R. de l'Abbé Sauvages
Théâtre Opéra
R. de la Madeleine
Maison romaine
Pl. aux Herbes
N.-Dame et St-Castor
Place Belle Croix
R. de la Curaterie
Pl. du Grand Temple
Grand Temple
Pl. du Chapitre
Ste-Eugénie
R. d. fr. Mineurs
Rue Porte de France
Rue Emile Jamais
St. Paul
R. Tedenat
R. du Château Fadaise
R. Delon Soubeyran
Rue Lecdelièvre
R. Gergonne
R. Maubet
Rue de l'Étoile
Rue Fresque
R. de Bernis
Rue de la Madeleine
R. des Marchands
Musée du Vieux Nîmes
R. du Chapitre
Rue Trelis
R. Poise
Bld. Amiral Courbet
R. Colbert
Rue Roussy
R. des Calquières
R. des Patins
Chlle. des Jésuites
Grand Rue
Musée archéologique
Rue Dorée
Hôtel de Ville
R. Grizot
R.d.l. Monnaie
Pl. du Marché
Pl. de l'Hôtel de Ville
R. des Greffes
R. des Fourbisseurs
Pl. de la Salamandre
R. St-Yon
Rue de la Pitié
R. St-Antoine
R. des Arènes
R.d.l. Violette
R. l'Aspic
R. des Chapeliers
R. Régale
Musée Taurin
Boulevard des Arènes
Square de la Couronne
Rue Notre Dame
Rue Bigot
Rue Reboul
Arènes
Palais de Justice
Boulevard de la Libération
Boulevard de Prague
Petite Rue du Louvre
Ste-Perpétue
Temple de l'Oratoire
Rue Porte de France
R. Ste-Ursule
Rue Jean Reboul
Place des Arènes
Esplanade Ch. de Gaulle
Fontaine Pradier
Rue Monjardin
R. A. Ducros
Boulevard des Arènes
Rue de l'Hôtel-Dieu
R. Villeperdrix
Square du 11 Novembre
Bld. de Bruxelles
Rue de Pradier
Rue du Mail
Porte de France
Pl. de la Porte de France
Rue de la République
Rue Cart
Rue de la Cité Foulc
R. Bridaine
Chapelle
Avenue Feuchères
R. Pécolet
Rue de la Servie
R. de Chaffoy
Rue du Cirque Romain
Place Montcalm
Rue Bourdaloue
R. L. Guiraud
Rue Briconnet
R. Du Guesclin
R. Jeanne d'Arc
R. Bayard
Rue de la République
R. Pharamond
Rue Suger
Rue de St-Gilles
Musée des Beaux-Arts
Rue Aton
Pl. Du Guesclin
Rue Bernard
Préfecture
Rue Marc
NÎMES
Rue de Générac
Rue Massillon
Rue Rivarol
Rue Ruffi
Pl. du 8 Mai 45
R. Court de Gebelin
Rue Guillemette
R. Raymond
R. Scatisse
Boulevard Talabot
Bld. Sgt. Triaire
N
0
250m
0
250 yd

INDEX

Abbaye du Thoronet 63
Aigues-Mortes 43
Aix-en-Provence 46–48
Antibes 67–69
Apt 32
Arles 37–41
Avignon 13–16
Bandol 53
Baux-de-Provence 26–28
Beaulieu-sur-Mer 78
Biot 67
Bonnieux 29–30
Bormes-les-Mimosas 59
Cagnes-sur-Mer 72–73
Calanques 52
Camargue 41–42
Cannes 65–66
Cap Canaille 53
Cap Ferrat 78
Carpentras 19–20
Cassis 53
Châteauneuf-du-Pape 16
Colorado 32
Corniche d'Or 63
Corniches 76–79
Côte Bleue 45–46
Eze 78
Fontaine-de-Vaucluse 21
Fontvieille 28
Forcalquier 33–34
Fréjus 61–63
Frioul, îles du 52
Ganagobie 34
Gordes 31
Gorges du Loup 71
Gorges du Verdon 35
Grasse 69–70
Hyères 55–56
Iles d'Hyères 56–57
Juan-les-Pins 67–69
La-Colle-sur-Loup 71–72
Lacoste 29
La Turbie 79
Le Lavandou 59
Lérins, îles de 66
L'Esterel 63
Levant, île du 57
L'Isle-sur-la-Sorgue 21
Lourmarin 30–31
Manosque 32–33
Marseille 48–52
Massif des Maures 61
Ménerbes 29
Menton 79–80
Monaco 80–83
Monte-Carlo 82–83
Mont Ventoux 19
Mougins 66–67
Moustiers-Sainte-Marie 34–35
Nice 73–76
Nîmes 21–23
Oppède-le-Vieux 29
Orange 16–18
Pays des Ocres 31–32
Pernes-les-Fontaines 20–21
Petit Luberon 29–31
Pont du Gard 23
Porquerolles 56–57
Port-Cros 57
Port-Grimaud 61
Roquebrune 79
Roquemaure 16
Roussillon 32
Saint-Gilles 41
Saint-Paul-de-Vence 71
Saint-Raphaël 61–63
Saint-Rémy-de-Provence 25–26
Saint-Tropez 59–61
Sainte-Baume 54
Sainte-Maxime 61
Sainte-Victoire 48
Saintes-Maries 42–43
Salon de Provence 45
Sault 19
Sénanque 31
Silvacane 31
Tarascon 28
Toulon 54–55
Vaison-la-Romaine 18–19
Vallauris 67
Vallée des Paillons 79
Vence 71
Villefranche-sur-Mer 76–78

General Editor
Barbara Ender-Jones
English Adaptation
Judith Farr
Barbara Ender-Jones
Layout
Alain Piccard
Photo credits
Claude Hervé-Bazin;
Huber/Gräfenhain, pp. 10–11, 30;
Huber/Panci, p. 64
Drawing
Sofie Czaplejewicz
Maps
Elsner & Schichor;
JPM Publications

Copyright © 2003
JPM Publications S.A.
12, avenue William-Fraisse,
1006 Lausanne, Suisse
information@jpmguides.com
http://www.jpmguides.com/

All rights reserved. No part of this book may be reproduced or transmitted in any form or by any means, electronic or mechanical, including photocopying, recording or by any information storage and retrieval system without permission in writing from the publisher.

Every care has been taken to verify the information in the guide, but neither the publisher nor his client can accept responsibility for any errors that may have occurred. If you spot an inaccuracy or a serious omission, please let us know.

Printed in Switzerland
Weber/Bienne (CTP) — 03/05/01
Edition 2003–2004

HAUTE-PROVENCE
N
0
20 km
GREAT BRITAIN
BELGIUM
GERMANY
LUXEMBOURG
FRANCE
SWITZERLAND
Provence
ITALY
ANDORRA
SPAIN
DRÔME
HAUTES-ALPES
VAUCLUSE
LANGUEDOC-ROUSSILLON
ALPES-DE-HAUTE-PROVENCE
ALPES-MARITIMES
ITALY
Baix
Crest
Châtillon-en-Diois
Agnières-en-Devoluy
St-Laurent-du-Cros
Merlette
Orcières
St-Clément
Guillestre
Ceillac
St-Véran
Savigliano
Aubenas
Sauzet
Luc-en-Diois
La Cluse
St-Julien-en-Beauchêne
La Bâtie-Neuve
Parc National des Ecrins
Parc du Queyras
Risoul
Vars
Pontechianale
Casteldelfino
Fossano
Le Teil
Montélimar
Bourdeaux
La Beaume
Gap
Chorges
Embrun
Villeneuve-de-Berg
Dieulefit
La Motte-Chalancon
Aspres-sur Buëch
Veynes
Lac de Serre-Ponçon
Savines-le-Lac
Les Orres
St-Paul-sur-Ubaye
Ubaye
Accéglio
Viviers
Donzère
Tallard
Remollon
Larche
Ruoms
Vallon-Pont-d'Arc
Grignan
Rémuzat
L'Epine
Serres
La Saulce
St-Vincent-l.-F.
Revel
Jausiers
Argentera
Cúneo
Pierrelatte
Sahune
Rosans
Le Monétier-Allemont
Durance
Barcelonnette
Valréas
Nyons
Orpierre
Larange-Montéglin
La Motte-du-Caire
Sasse
Seyne-les-Alpes
Pra-Loup
Les Agneliers-Bas
Borgo S. Dalmazzo
Vinádio
Demonte
Ardèche
Rhône
Bollène
Barret-le-Bas
Les Monges 2116 m
La Foux-d'Allos
Mont Pelat 3053 m
Le Pra
Barjac
Tulette
Vaison-la-Romaine
Buis-les-Baronnies
Ouvèze
Col de la Cayolle
Auron
Terme di Valdieri
Pont-St-Esprit
Barles
Le Vernet
Allos
Alpes Maritimes
Isola
Vanson
Bès
Buëch
Colmars
Parc National du Mercantour
Isola 2000
Cèze
Séguret
Sablet
Séderon
Sisteron
La Javie
Tinée
Cime du Gélas 3143 m
Violès
Mont Ventoux 1909 m
Malaucène
Montbrun-les-Bains
St-Vincent-sur-J.
Montagne du Cheval Blanc 2323 m
Entraunes
Bagnols-sur-Cèze
Orange
Gigondas
Volonne
Thorame-Haute
Guillaumes
Valberg
Tende
Sarrians
Revest-du-Bion
Digne-les-Bains
Beuil
St-Sauveur-sur-Tinée
St-Martin-Vésubie
Roquemaure
Châteauneuf-du-Pape
Carpentras
Sault
St-Etienne-les-Orgues
Cruis
Malijai
Bléone
Marie
Uzès
Sorgues
Pernes-les-Fontaines
St-Christol
Banon
Châteauredon
Gorges de Daluis
Gorges du Cians
Lantosque
Saorge
Pont du Gard
AVIGNON
Le Pontet
Venasque
Simiane-la-Rotonde
Les Mées
Mézel
St-André-les-Alpes
Annot
Puget-Théniers
Villars-sur-Var
Remoulins
Villeneuve-lès-Avignon
L'Isle-sur-la-Sorgue
Fontaine-de-Vaucluse
Abbaye de Sénanque
St-Saturnin-lès-Apt
Forcalquier
Lurs
Asse
Barrême
Var
St-Jean-la-Rivière
Peira-Cava
Breil-sur-Roya
Gardon
Calavon
Largue
Bras-d'Asse
Alpes de Provence
Entrevaux
NÎMES
Châteaurenard
Gordes
Reillanne
Oraison
Roquesteron
Redessan
Noves
Roussillon
Apt
Céreste
Voix
Lac de Castillon
Estéron
Sospel
Cavaillon
Moustiers-Ste-Marie
Castellane
L'Escarène
Beaucaire
Tarascon
St-Rémy-de-Provence
Ménerbes
Coulon
Bonnieux
Parc du Lubéron
Manosque
Valensole
Riez
Le Palud-sur-Verdon
St-Martin-du-Var
Roquebrune-Cap-Martin
Ventimiglia
Montagne du Luberon
Lourmarin
Cucuron
Grambois
Gréoux-les-Bains
Colostre
Lac de Ste-Croix
Allemagne-en-Provence
Grand Canyon du Verdon
Le Logis-du-Pin
Gréolières
Coursegoules
MONACO
Menton
Monte Carlo
Garons
Plan-d'Orgon
Chaîne des Alpilles
Loup
A 7
A 9
A51
A54
A8
N7
N86
N75
N85
N94
D994
D900B
D900
N96
N202
N204
D2
D22
N100
N570
D99

PROVENCE/CÔTE D'AZUR
0
20 km
N
NÎMES
AVIGNON
Châteaurenard
Noves
L'Isle-sur-la-Sorgue
Fontaine-de-Vaucluse
Gordes
Roussillon
VAUCLUSE
Reillanne
Céreste
Apt
Cavaillon
Ménerbes
Bonnieux
Montagne du Luberon
Parc du Luberon
Lourmarin
Cucuron
Grambois
Manosque
Redessan
Beaucaire
Tarascon
St-Rémy-de-Provence
Plan-d'Orgon
Garons
Bellegarde
Les Baux
Chaîne des Alpilles
387 m
Abbaye de Montmajour
Maussane
Eyguières
Abbaye de Silvacane
Pont-Royal
Cadenet
Pertuis
Mirabeau
Vauvert
St-Gilles
Arles
BOUCHES-DU-RHÔNE
Salon-de-Provence
Rognes
Lambesc
Le Puy-Ste-Réparade
Peyrolles-en-Provence
Meyrargues
Albaron
St-Martin-de-Crau
Miramas
St-Cannat
Parc Naturel Régional de Camargue
Camargue
Petit Rhône
Mas Thibert
Sylvéréal
Étang de Vaccarès
Le Sambuc
Istres
Berre-l'Etang
Étang de Berre
Vitrolles
Vauvenargues
Aix-en-Provence
St-Pilon 994 m
Pourrières
Rousset
Saintes-Maries-de-la-Mer
Golfe de Beauduc
Port-St-Louis-du-Rhône
Port-de-Bouc
Martigues
Marignane
Gardanne
Trets
Pte. du Sablon
Golfe de Fos
Châteauneuf-lès-Martigues
Septèmes-les-Vallons
Auriol
Carro
Sausset-les-Pins
Carry-le-Rouet
Allauch
Roquevaire
Bouches du Rhône
Château d'If
Aubagne
Gémenos
Iles du Frioul
MARSEILLE
Cassis
La Ciotat
Cap de l'Aigle
Mer Méditerranée
Oraison
Voix
Valensole
Riez
Bras-d'Asse
Gréoux-les-Bains
Allemagne-en-Provence
Lac de Ste-Croix
Moustiers-Ste-Marie
Le Palud-sur-Verdon
Grand Canyon du Verdon
Alpes de Provence
Lac de Castillon
Castellane
Ginasservis
Rians
Varages
Montmeyan
Aups
Comps-sur-Artuby
Sillans-la-Cascade
Barjols
VAR
Salernes
Cotignac
St-Maximin-la-Ste-Baume
Carcès
Lorgues
Abbaye du Thoronet
Le Val
Tourves
Rougiers
Brignoles
Cabasse
Le Luc
Vidauban
Les Arcs
Draguignan
Le Muy
Plan-d'Aups-Ste-Baume
Massif de la Sainte Baume
Garéoult
Besse-sur-Issole
Flassans-sur-Issole
Forcalqueiret
Gonfaron
Méounes-les-Montrieux
Signes
Cuges-les-Pins
Le Beausset
Mont Caume 801 m
Cuers
Pierrefeu-du-Var
Collobrières
Massif des Maures
Les Lecques
St-Cyr-s.-Mer
La Valette-du-Var.
Bandol
Sanary-sur-Mer
Six Fours-les-Plages
TOULON
Les Sablettes
Cap Sicié
St-Mandrier-s.-Mer
Cap Cépet
Carqueiranne
Hyères
La Londe-les-Maures
Hyères-Plage
La Tour-Fondue
Giens
I. de Porquerolles
Porquerolles
Port-Cros
I. de Port-Cros
Héliopolis
I. du Levant
Iles d'Hyères (Iles d'Or)
Bormes-les-Mimosas
Le Lavandou
Cap Bénat
Cavalière
Le Rayol
Cavalaire-sur-Mer
Cap Lardier
Cap Cartaya
Cap Camarat
La Croix-Valmer
La Môle
Cogolin
Grimaud
La Garde-Freinet
St-Tropez
Cap de St-Tropez
Ste-Maxime
Les Issambres
St-Aygulf
Fréjus
St-Raphaël
Agay
Massif de l'Esterel
Mandelieu-la-Napoule
CANNES
Ile Ste Marguerite
Ile St. Honorat
Golfe-Juan
Cap d'Antibes
Antibes
Vallauris
Mougins
Grasse
Lac de St. Cassien
Callas
Fayence
Montferrat
St-Cézaire-s.-Siagne
Mons
St-Vallier-de-Thiey
Gourdon
Le Logis-du-Pin
ALPES-MARITIMES
Gréolières
Coursegoules
Vence
Le Bar-sur-Loup
St-Paul
Cagnes-s.-M.
NICE
Cap Ferrat
Villefranche-s.-M.
Beaulieu-s.-M.
MONACO
Monte Carlo Monaco
Roquebrune-Cap-Martin
Menton
St-Martin-du-Var
Roquesteron
St-Jean-la-Rivière
L'Escarène
Sospel
Estéron
Loup
Cagne
Real Collobrier
Argens
Aille
Nartuby
Artuby
Verdon
Colostre
Durance
Coulon
Rhône
Gardon
A 9
A 7
A 54
A 51
A 8
A 52
A 50
A 57
N100
N96
N113
N568
N570
N560
N 7
N 8
N7
N98
N85
N202
D22
D99
D559
D2
GREAT BRITAIN
GERMANY
BELGIUM
LUXEMBOURG
FRANCE
SWITZERLAND
ITALY
Provence
ANDORRA
SPAIN